TACO
TUESDAY

Publications International, Ltd.

Pictured on the back cover *(left to right)*: Mexican-Style Corn on the Cob *(page 148)*, Fish Tacos with Citrus Pineapple Salsa *(page 94)*, and Beer-Braised Spicy Beef Tacos *(page 96)*.

ISBN: 978-1-60822-486-3

Library of Congress Control Number: 2016936140

Manufactured in China.

8 7 6 5 4 3 2 1

Microwave Cooking: Microwave ovens vary in wattage. Use the cooking times as guidelines and check for doneness before adding more time.

Preparation/Cooking Times: Preparation times are based on the approximate amount of time required to assemble the recipe before cooking, baking, chilling or serving. These times include preparation steps such as measuring, chopping and mixing. The fact that some preparations and cooking can be done simultaneously is taken into account. Preparation of optional ingredients and serving suggestions is not included.

Publications International, Ltd.

TACO TUESDAY

TABLE OF CONTENTS

PARTY STARTERS
4

BRUNCH BAKES & TASTES
36

NEVER ENOUGH TACOS
60

DINNER WINNERS
104

SIMPLE SIDES
148

SATISFYING SWEETS
174

INDEX & ACKNOWLEDGMENTS
187

PARTY STARTERS

MINI BEEF TOSTADAS

MAKES 4 DOZEN TOSTADAS

1 pound ground beef

1 tablespoon instant minced onion

1 can (8 ounces) refried beans

1 can (4 ounces) chopped green chiles, drained (optional)

½ cup bottled taco sauce

48 round tortilla chips

1 cup (4 ounces) shredded Cheddar cheese

1 Preheat oven to 375°F. Brown beef and onion in large skillet over medium heat 6 to 8 minutes; drain fat.

2 Add beans, chiles, if desired, and taco sauce; cook and stir about 4 minutes or until bubbly. Spoon about 1 heaping tablespoon beef mixture onto each tortilla chip; sprinkle with cheese. Place on baking sheets.

3 Bake 2 minutes or until cheese is melted.

TACO POPCORN OLÉ

MAKES 6 SERVINGS

9 cups air-popped popcorn

Butter-flavored cooking spray

1 teaspoon chili powder

½ teaspoon salt

½ teaspoon garlic powder

⅛ teaspoon ground red pepper (optional)

1 Preheat oven to 350°F. Line 15×10×1-inch jelly-roll pan with foil.

2 Place popcorn in single layer in prepared pan. Spray with cooking spray.

3 Combine chili powder, salt, garlic powder and red pepper, if desired, in small bowl. Sprinkle over popcorn; toss lightly to coat.

4 Bake 5 minutes or until heated through, stirring gently after 3 minutes. Spread popcorn in single layer on large sheet of foil to cool.

TIPS

Store popcorn in tightly covered container at room temperature up to 4 days.

For a spicier version, substitute a hot Mexican-style chili powder or a chipotle chili powder for the regular chili powder, or add ground red pepper.

TORTILLA "PIZZAS"

MAKES 8 SERVINGS

1 can (about 14 ounces) Mexican-style stewed tomatoes, drained

1 can (10 ounces) chunk white chicken packed in water, drained

1 green onion, minced

2 teaspoons ground cumin, divided

½ teaspoon garlic powder

1 cup fat-free refried beans

4 tablespoons chopped fresh cilantro, divided

2 large flour tortillas *or* 4 small flour tortillas

1 cup (4 ounces) shredded Monterey Jack cheese with jalapeño peppers

1 Preheat broiler. Combine tomatoes, chicken, green onion, 1 teaspoon cumin and garlic powder in medium bowl. Mix well; set aside.

2 Combine beans, remaining 1 teaspoon cumin and 2 tablespoons cilantro in small bowl. Set aside.

3 Place tortillas on baking sheet. Broil 30 seconds per side or until crisp but not browned. Remove from oven. *Reduce oven temperature to 400°F.* Spread bean mixture evenly over each tortilla. Top with chicken mixture and cheese. Bake 5 minutes.

4 *Turn oven to broil.* Broil tortillas 2 to 3 minutes or until cheese melts. Do not let tortilla edges burn. Top with remaining cilantro. Serve immediately.

MINI TACO QUICHES

MAKES 12 SERVINGS | PREP TIME 20 MINUTES **COOK TIME** 30 MINUTES

1 pound lean ground beef

⅓ cup chopped onions

⅓ cup sliced black olives

1 can (8 ounces) tomato sauce

1 package (1¼ ounces) taco
    seasoning mix

2 tablespoons FRANK'S® RedHot®
    Original Cayenne Pepper
    Sauce

1 egg, beaten

4 flour tortillas (10 inches)

⅓ cup sour cream

½ cup (2 ounces) shredded
    Cheddar cheese

PREHEAT oven to 350°F. Grease 12 muffin pan cups. Set aside.

COOK beef and onions in large nonstick skillet until meat is browned; drain. Remove from heat. Stir in olives, tomato sauce, *¼ cup* water, taco seasoning, **FRANK'S RedHot** Sauce and egg; mix well.

CUT each flour tortilla into 3 rounds, using 4-inch cookie cutter. Fit tortilla rounds into prepared muffin cups. Fill each tortilla cup with *¼ cup* meat mixture. Top each with sour cream and cheese.

BAKE 25 minutes or until heated through.

7-LAYER DIP

MAKES 10 SERVINGS

1 package (3 ounces) ramen noodles, any flavor, crushed*

2 tablespoons dried taco seasoning mix

3 ripe avocados, diced

1 jalapeño pepper, finely chopped**

2 tablespoons finely chopped fresh cilantro

2 tablespoons lime juice

1 clove garlic, minced

½ teaspoon salt

1 can (about 15 ounces) refried beans

1 container (16 ounces) sour cream

2 cups (8 ounces) shredded Mexican Cheddar-Jack cheese

2 medium tomatoes, diced

3 green onions, thinly sliced

Tortilla chips

*Discard seasoning packet.

**Jalapeño peppers can sting and irritate the skin, so wear rubber gloves when handling peppers and do not touch your eyes.

1 Combine noodles and seasoning mix in medium bowl; mix well.

2 Mash avocados, jalapeño pepper, cilantro, lime juice, garlic and salt in large bowl.

3 Spread refried beans in bottom of 8-inch glass baking dish. Layer sour cream, noodles, avocado mixture, cheese, tomatoes and green onions evenly over beans. Serve immediately or cover and refrigerate for up to 8 hours. Serve with tortilla chips.

MEXICAN TORTILLA STACKS

MAKES 16 SERVINGS | PREP TIME 10 MINUTES
START TO FINISH 20 MINUTES

½ cup ORTEGA® Salsa, any variety, divided

½ cup finely chopped cooked chicken

¼ cup sour cream

8 (8-inch) ORTEGA® Flour Soft Tortillas

½ cup prepared guacamole

⅓ cup ORTEGA® Refried Beans

6 tablespoons (1½ ounces) shredded Cheddar cheese

Additional sour cream and chopped cilantro (optional)

HEAT oven to 350°F. Mix ¼ cup salsa, chicken and ¼ cup sour cream in small bowl.

PLACE 2 tortillas on ungreased cookie sheet; spread each with salsa-chicken mixture. Spread 2 more tortillas with guacamole and place on top of salsa-chicken mixture.

MIX refried beans with remaining ¼ cup salsa; spread onto 2 more tortillas and place on top of guacamole. Top each stack with remaining 2 tortillas; sprinkle with cheese.

BAKE 8 to 10 minutes until cheese is melted and filling is hot.

TOP with sour cream and cilantro, if desired. Cut each stack into 8 wedges.

NOTE

Prepared guacamole can be found in the refrigerated or frozen food sections at most supermarkets.

CLASSIC GUACAMOLE

MAKES ABOUT 2 CUPS

4 tablespoons finely chopped white onion, divided

1 to 2 serrano or jalapeño peppers,* seeded and finely chopped

1½ tablespoons coarsely chopped fresh cilantro, divided

¼ teaspoon chopped garlic (optional)

2 large ripe avocados

1 medium tomato, peeled and chopped

1 to 2 teaspoons fresh lime juice

¼ teaspoon salt

Corn Tortilla Chips (recipe follows) or packaged corn tortilla chips

Serrano and jalapeño peppers can sting and irritate the skin, so wear rubber gloves when handling peppers and do not touch your eyes.

1 Combine 2 tablespoons onion, serrano, 1 tablespoon cilantro and garlic, if desired, in large mortar. Grind with pestle until almost smooth. (Mixture can be processed in food processor, if necessary, but it may become more watery than desired.)

2 Cut avocados into halves; remove and discard pits. Scoop out pulp; place in large bowl. Add serrano mixture; mash roughly, leaving avocado slightly chunky.

3 Add tomato, lime juice, salt, remaining 2 tablespoons onion and ½ tablespoon cilantro to avocado mixture; mix well. Serve immediately with Corn Tortilla Chips or cover and refrigerate up to 4 hours.

CORN TORTILLA CHIPS

MAKES 6 DOZEN

12 (6-inch) corn tortillas, day-old*

Vegetable oil

½ to 1 teaspoon salt

If tortillas are fresh, let stand, uncovered, in single layer on wire rack 1 to 2 hours to dry slightly.

1 Stack 6 tortillas. Cutting through stack, cut into 6 equal wedges. Repeat with remaining tortillas.

2 Heat ½ inch oil in large heavy skillet over medium-high heat to 375°F; adjust heat to maintain temperature.

3 Fry tortilla wedges in single layer 1 minute or until crisp, turning occasionally. Remove and drain on paper towels. Sprinkle chips with salt. Repeat with remaining wedges.

PARTY STARTERS

EASY EMPANADAS

MAKES 12 EMPANADAS | PREP TIME 10 MINUTES **START TO FINISH** 25 MINUTES

1 cup prepared refrigerated
    barbecued shredded pork

2 tablespoons ORTEGA® Taco
    Sauce, any variety

1 tablespoon ORTEGA® Fire-
    Roasted Diced Green Chiles

1 can (12 count) refrigerated
    biscuits

1 egg, well beaten

1 cup ORTEGA® Black Bean & Corn
    Salsa

PREHEAT oven to 375°F. Mix pork, taco sauce and chiles in small bowl.

SEPARATE biscuits into 12 pieces. Flatten each biscuit into 6-inch round, using rolling pin. Divide filling evenly among biscuits, spreading over half of each round to within ¼ inch of edge. Fold dough over filling; press edges with fork to seal well. Place on ungreased cookie sheet. Brush tops with beaten egg.

BAKE 12 to 15 minutes or until edges are golden brown. Immediately remove from cookie sheet. Serve warm with salsa for dipping.

FESTIVE TACO CUPS

MAKES 24 TACO CUPS

1 tablespoon vegetable oil

½ cup chopped onion

½ pound ground turkey or ground beef

1 clove garlic, minced

½ teaspoon dried oregano

½ teaspoon chili powder or taco seasoning mix

¼ teaspoon salt

1¼ cups (5 ounces) shredded taco cheese or Mexican cheese blend, divided

1 can (11½ ounces) refrigerated corn breadstick dough

Chopped fresh tomato and sliced green onion (optional)

1 Heat oil in large skillet over medium heat. Add onion; cook until tender. Add turkey; cook and stir until turkey is no longer pink. Stir in garlic, oregano, chili powder and salt. Remove from heat and stir in ½ cup cheese; set aside.

2 Preheat oven to 375°F. Lightly grease 24 mini (1¾-inch) muffin cups. Remove dough from container but do not unroll dough. Separate dough into 8 pieces at perforations. Divide each piece into 3 pieces; roll or pat each piece into 3-inch circle. Press circles into prepared muffin cups.

3 Fill each cup with 1½ to 2 teaspoons turkey mixture. Bake 10 minutes. Sprinkle tops of taco cups with remaining ¾ cup cheese; bake 2 to 3 minutes more or until cheese is melted. Garnish with tomato and green onion.

FESTIVE TACO NACHOS

MAKES 8 SERVINGS | PREP TIME 5 MINUTES **COOK TIME** 20 MINUTES **BAKE TIME** 5 MINUTES

2 pounds ground beef

1 jar (16 ounces) PACE® Picante Sauce

8 ounces tortilla chips

4 cups shredded Mexican blend **or** shredded Cheddar Jack cheese (about 16 ounces)

Chopped tomato

Sliced pitted ripe olives

Sliced green onions

1 Heat the oven to 350°F.

2 Cook the beef in a 12-inch skillet over medium-high heat until well browned, stirring often to separate the meat.

3 Stir the picante sauce in the skillet and heat to a boil. Reduce the heat to low. Cook for 5 minutes or until the beef is cooked through.

4 Arrange the tortilla chips on **2** (12-inch) aluminum pizza pans. Top with the beef mixture and cheese. Bake for 5 minutes or until the cheese is melted. Top with the tomato, olives and onions.

LAYERED MEXICAN DIP

MAKES 10 SERVINGS

1 package (8 ounces) cream cheese, softened

1 tablespoon plus 1 teaspoon taco seasoning mix

1 cup canned black beans

1 cup salsa

1 cup shredded lettuce

1 cup (4 ounces) shredded Cheddar cheese

½ cup chopped green onions

2 tablespoons sliced pitted black olives

Tortilla chips

1 Combine cream cheese and seasoning mix in small bowl. Spread on bottom of 9-inch pie plate.

2 Layer black beans, salsa, lettuce, cheese, green onions and olives over cream cheese mixture. Refrigerate until ready to serve. Serve with tortilla chips.

EASY TACO DIP

MAKES ABOUT 3 CUPS

½ pound ground beef

1 cup frozen corn

½ cup chopped onion

½ cup salsa

½ cup mild taco sauce

1 can (4 ounces) diced mild green chiles, drained

1 can (4 ounces) sliced black olives, drained

1 cup (4 ounces) shredded Mexican cheese blend

Sour cream (optional)

Tortilla chips

SLOW COOKER DIRECTIONS

1 Brown beef in large skillet over medium-high heat 6 to 8 minutes, stirring to break up meat. Drain fat. Transfer beef to slow cooker.

2 Add corn, onion, salsa, taco sauce, chiles and olives to slow cooker; mix well. Cover; cook on LOW 2 to 3 hours.

3 Just before serving, stir in cheese blend. Top with sour cream, if desired. Serve with tortilla chips.

TIP

To keep this dip hot through an entire party, simply leave it in the slow cooker on LOW or WARM.

TACO CHEESE BALLS

MAKES 24 BALLS | PREP TIME 10 MINUTES **START TO FINISH** 50 MINUTES

1 package (8 ounces) cream cheese, softened

4 ounces goat cheese, softened

1 packet (1.25 ounces) ORTEGA® Taco Seasoning Mix, divided

6 ORTEGA® Yellow Corn Taco Shells

COMBINE cheeses and 2 tablespoons taco seasoning mix in medium bowl. Mix well; place in refrigerator 10 minutes to make rolling cheese into balls easier.

PLACE taco shells in food processor; pulse several minutes to crush into consistency of large bread crumbs. Place crumbs in small bowl. In separate small bowl, add remaining taco seasoning mix.

REMOVE cheese mixture from refrigerator and roll into quarter-size balls. Roll balls in taco seasoning mix, then in the crushed taco shells. Place balls on plate and, once all balls have been made, place in refrigerator to chill at least 30 minutes or up to 2 hours before serving.

TIP

Try dipping the balls into ORTEGA® Taco Sauce for added flavor.

TEX-MEX GUACAMOLE PLATTER

MAKES 6 TO 8 SERVINGS

4 ripe avocados

¼ cup fresh lime juice

2 tablespoons olive oil

3 cloves garlic, crushed

½ teaspoon salt

¼ teaspoon black pepper

1 cup (4 ounces) shredded Colby Jack cheese

1 cup diced seeded plum tomatoes

⅓ cup sliced pitted black olives

⅓ cup salsa

1 tablespoon minced fresh cilantro

Tortilla chips

1 Cut avocados in half; remove pits. Scoop out pulp into food processor. Add lime juice, oil, garlic, salt and pepper. Cover; process until almost smooth.

2 Spread avocado mixture evenly on large dinner plate or serving platter, leaving border around edge. Top with cheese, tomatoes, olives, salsa and cilantro. Serve with tortilla chips.

BITE SIZE TACOS

MAKES 8 APPETIZER SERVINGS | PREP TIME 5 MINUTES **COOK TIME** 15 MINUTES

1 pound ground beef

1 package (1.25 ounces) taco seasoning mix

2 cups FRENCH'S® French Fried Onions

¼ cup chopped fresh cilantro

32 bite-size round tortilla chips

¾ cup sour cream

1 cup (4 ounces) shredded Cheddar cheese

1 Cook beef in nonstick skillet over medium-high heat 5 minutes or until browned; drain. Stir in taco seasoning mix, *¾ cup* water, *1 cup* French Fried Onions and cilantro. Simmer 5 minutes or until flavors are blended, stirring often.

2 Preheat oven to 350°F. Arrange tortilla chips on foil-lined baking sheet. Top with beef mixture, sour cream, remaining onions and cheese.

3 Bake 5 minutes or until cheese is melted and onions are golden.

TACO DIP

MAKES 10 SERVINGS

12 ounces cream cheese, softened

½ cup sour cream

2 teaspoons chili powder

1½ teaspoons ground cumin

⅛ teaspoon ground red pepper

½ cup salsa

1 cup (4 ounces) shredded Cheddar cheese

1 cup (4 ounces) shredded Monterey Jack cheese

½ cup diced plum tomatoes

⅓ cup sliced green onions

¼ cup sliced pitted black olives

¼ cup sliced pimiento-stuffed green olives

Shredded lettuce

Tortilla chips and blue corn chips

1 Combine cream cheese, sour cream, chili powder, cumin and red pepper in large bowl; mix until well blended. Stir in salsa.

2 Spread dip onto serving platter. Top with cheeses, tomatoes, green onions and olives. Sprinkle shredded lettuce around edges of dip.

3 Serve with tortilla chips and blue corn chips.

BUFFALO GUACAMOLE

MAKES 1½ CUPS | PREP TIME 15 MINUTES

2 small ripe avocados, halved, pitted and peeled

3 tablespoons FRANK'S® RedHot® Original Cayenne Pepper Sauce

3 tablespoons minced fresh cilantro leaves

3 tablespoons lime or lemon juice

1 clove garlic, minced

½ teaspoon salt

Tortilla chips (optional)

COARSELY mash avocados in medium bowl. Stir in remaining ingredients; mix well. Chill if desired. Serve with tortilla chips.

NUMBER ONE NACHOS

MAKES 8 SERVINGS | PREP TIME 10 MINUTES **COOK TIME** 15 MINUTES

- 1 pound lean ground beef
- 1 packet (1.25 ounces) taco seasoning mix
- ½ cup water
- ½ cup HEINZ® Tomato Ketchup
- 1 package (8 ounces) tortilla chips
- ½ cup shredded Cheddar cheese
- ½ cup diced fresh tomato

1 In a medium skillet, brown beef until thoroughly cooked, 5 to 6 minutes. Drain fat.

2 Stir in seasoning mix and water and simmer 2 minutes or until slightly thickened. Stir in Ketchup and heat.

3 Place chips in a baking dish, overlapping chips slightly. Top chips with beef mixture. Sprinkle with cheese.

4 Bake in 400°F oven, 3 to 5 minutes to melt cheese. Top with diced tomato.

BRUNCH BAKES & TASTES

BREAKFAST TACOS

MAKES 2 SERVINGS

6 mini taco shells *or* 2 regular taco shells

2 eggs

½ teaspoon taco seasoning mix

2 tablespoons shredded Cheddar cheese or cheese sauce

2 tablespoons mild salsa

2 tablespoons chopped fresh parsley

Sliced green onion and shredded lettuce (optional)

1 Heat taco shells according to package directions.

2 Meanwhile, beat eggs in small bowl until well blended. Spray small nonstick skillet with nonstick cooking spray; heat over medium-low heat. Pour eggs into skillet; cook and stir until desired doneness. Sprinkle with seasoning mix.

3 Spoon eggs into taco shells. Top each taco with 1 teaspoon each cheese, salsa and parsley. Add green onion and lettuce, if desired.

TORTILLA FRITTATA

MAKES 6 TO 8 SERVINGS | PREP TIME 20 MINUTES **START TO FINISH** 40 MINUTES

8 eggs

1 cup ORTEGA® Salsa, any variety

½ teaspoon salt

½ teaspoon black pepper

4 ORTEGA® Yellow Corn Taco Shells or Whole Grain Corn Taco Shells, crushed

1 tablespoon vegetable oil

1 cup chopped mushrooms

½ cup chopped tomato

½ cup chopped green onions

1½ cups shredded taco cheese blend

COMBINE eggs, salsa, salt and pepper in large bowl; mix well. Crumble taco shells over egg mixture and let soak 10 minutes.

PREHEAT oven to 400°F.

HEAT oil in ovenproof skillet over medium-high heat. Add mushrooms, tomato and green onions; cook and stir 4 minutes.

SPREAD ingredients evenly around skillet. Pour in egg mixture and spread out evenly in skillet. Cook about 2 minutes or until eggs begin to set around sides. Remove skillet from heat and sprinkle cheese over top.

BAKE 10 minutes or until frittata begins to puff up and brown.

SERVE frittata from skillet or transfer to serving plate and cut into wedges.

TIP

For a great presentation, bring the frittata to the table garnished with cilantro, sour cream and ORTEGA® Guacamole Style Dip.

MEXICAN BREAKFAST BURRITO

MAKES 4 SERVINGS

1 container (16 ounces) cholesterol-free egg substitute

⅛ teaspoon black pepper

⅓ cup canned black beans, rinsed and drained

2 tablespoons sliced green onions

2 (10-inch) flour tortillas

3 tablespoons shredded Cheddar cheese

3 tablespoons salsa

1 Whisk egg substitute and pepper in medium bowl until well blended. Spray large nonstick skillet with nonstick cooking spray; heat over medium heat. Pour egg mixture into skillet; cook 5 to 7 minutes or until mixture begins to set, stirring occasionally. Stir in beans and green onions; cook and stir 3 minutes or just until cooked through.

2 Spoon mixture evenly down centers of tortillas; top evenly with cheese. Roll up to enclose filling. Cut in half; top with salsa.

SPICY MEXICAN FRITTATA

MAKES 4 SERVINGS

1 jalapeño pepper*

1 clove garlic

1 medium tomato, peeled, halved, quartered and seeded

½ teaspoon ground coriander

½ teaspoon chili powder

½ cup chopped onion

1 cup frozen corn

6 egg whites

2 eggs

¼ cup fat-free (skim) milk

¼ teaspoon salt

¼ teaspoon black pepper

¼ cup (1 ounce) shredded part-skim farmer or mozzarella cheese

Jalapeño peppers can sting and irritate the skin, so wear rubber gloves when handling peppers and do not touch your eyes.

1 Place jalapeño pepper and garlic in food processor or blender. Cover; process until finely chopped. Add tomato, coriander and chili powder. Cover; process until tomato is almost smooth.

2 Spray large skillet with nonstick cooking spray; heat over medium heat until hot. Cook and stir onion until tender. Stir in tomato mixture and corn; cook 3 to 4 minutes or until liquid is almost evaporated, stirring occasionally.

3 Combine egg whites, eggs, milk, salt and black pepper in medium bowl. Add egg mixture all at once to skillet. Cook, without stirring, 2 minutes or until eggs begin to set. Run large spoon around edge of skillet, lifting eggs for even cooking. Remove skillet from heat when eggs are almost set but surface is still moist.

4 Sprinkle with cheese. Cover; let stand 3 to 4 minutes or until surface is set and cheese is melted. Cut into 4 wedges.

TORTILLA SCRAMBLE
WITH SALSA

MAKES 4 SERVINGS | PREP TIME 5 MINUTES **START TO FINISH** 10 MINUTES

8 eggs

¼ cup whipping cream or half-and-half

1 tablespoon butter

3 tablespoons ORTEGA® Salsa, any variety

1 cup broken ORTEGA® Taco Shells

½ cup (2 ounces) shredded Cheddar cheese

SUGGESTED TOPPINGS
Tortilla chips, chopped parsley, ORTEGA® Salsa

COMBINE eggs and whipping cream in mixing bowl. Beat with wire whisk.

MELT butter in heavy skillet. Add egg mixture and stir in 3 tablespoons salsa. Scramble eggs until they begin to set. Add broken taco shells and cheese, stirring to mix.

DIVIDE egg mixture evenly among individual plates.

TOP with tortilla chips, parsley and salsa, if desired.

SPANISH TORTILLA

MAKES 10 TO 12 SERVINGS

1 teaspoon olive oil

1 cup thinly sliced peeled potato

1 small zucchini, thinly sliced

¼ cup chopped onion

1 clove garlic, minced

1 cup shredded cooked chicken

8 eggs

½ teaspoon salt

½ teaspoon black pepper

¼ teaspoon red pepper flakes

Fresh tomato salsa (optional)

1 Heat oil in 10-inch nonstick skillet over medium-high heat. Add potato, zucchini, onion and garlic; cook and stir about 5 minutes or until potato is tender, turning frequently. Stir in chicken; cook 1 minute.

2 Meanwhile, whisk eggs, salt, black pepper and red pepper flakes in large bowl. Carefully pour egg mixture into skillet. Reduce heat to low. Cover and cook 12 to 15 minutes or until egg mixture is set in center.

3 Loosen edges of tortilla and slide onto large serving platter. Let stand 5 minutes before cutting into wedges or 1-inch cubes. Serve warm or at room temperature. Serve with salsa, if desired.

BRUNCH BAKES & TASTES

MEXICAN HASH BROWN BAKE

MAKES 12 SERVINGS | PREP TIME 15 MINUTES **START TO FINISH** 1 HOUR 10 MINUTES

Nonstick cooking spray

1 container (13 ounces) ORTEGA® Salsa & Cheese Bowl

1½ cups sour cream

1 can (4 ounces) ORTEGA® Fire-Roasted Diced Green Chiles or Diced Jalapeños

1 package (30 ounces) frozen shredded hash brown potatoes

2 ORTEGA® Taco Shells, any variety, coarsely crushed

PREHEAT oven to 350°F. Spray 13×9-inch baking dish with cooking spray.

COMBINE Salsa & Cheese, sour cream and chiles in large bowl; stir until blended. Gently stir in hash browns. Spoon mixture into baking dish.

SPRINKLE with crushed taco shells.

BAKE for 45 to 50 minutes or until bubbly around edges. Let stand for 5 minutes before serving.

TIP

Make this dish extra special by adding two sliced green onions or two slices crisp, crumbled bacon.

JOHNSONVILLE®
BREAKFAST EMPANADAS

MAKES 4 SERVINGS | PREP TIME 20 MINUTES **COOK TIME** 30 MINUTES

1 package (16 ounces) JOHNSONVILLE® Ground Sausage

5 eggs

1 cup sliced green onions

1 cup diced tomato

¾ cup milk, divided

1½ teaspoons chili seasoning

2 cups (8 ounces) shredded taco cheese

4 refrigerated pie crusts

1 egg yolk

1 teaspoon sugar

1 Preheat oven to 350°F. Brown sausage and crumble in skillet until cooked through; drain and reserve. Whisk eggs, green onions, tomatoes, ½ cup milk and chili seasoning. Pour into skillet; cook until creamy and slightly loose.

2 Place ¾ cup of egg mixture on half of one pie crust, leaving ½-inch border on edge. Top with ½ cup cheese and ½ cup of cooked sausage. Fold crust over mixture to form half circle and pinch edges with fork to seal. Make 3 (1-inch) slices on top to vent. Place on greased cookie sheet. Continue with remaining pie crusts.

3 Beat egg yolk, sugar and remaining ¼ cup milk in small bowl. Brush over empanadas. Bake for 30 minutes.

BREAKFAST TACO BAR

MAKES 7 TO 10 SERVINGS | PREP TIME 10 MINUTES **COOK TIME** 10 MINUTES

1 package (12 ounces) JOHNSONVILLE® Original Breakfast Sausage Links

14 (6-inch) flour tortillas

12 eggs

½ teaspoon salt

½ teaspoon black pepper

2 tablespoons vegetable oil

2 cups (8 ounces) shredded Cheddar cheese

2 medium tomatoes, chopped

Sour cream, salsa, chopped avocado or other toppings

1 Preheat oven to 200°F. Cook sausage according to package directions. Transfer to baking dish; cover and keep warm in oven. Wrap tortillas in foil; place in oven to warm through.

2 Whisk together eggs, salt and pepper in large bowl.

3 Heat oil in large skillet over medium heat. Add eggs; cook, without stirring, just until bottom is set. Gently bring edges to center, allowing uncooked eggs to reach pan bottom. Continue cooking and folding until set but still moist. Transfer to another baking dish; cover and keep warm in oven.

4 To serve, fill warm tortillas with spoonful of scrambled eggs and 2 sausage links. Top with cheese, tomatoes and other toppings, as desired.

BREAKFAST TAMALE PIE

MAKES 8 TO 12 SERVINGS | PREP TIME 15 MINUTES **START TO FINISH** 1 HOUR

1 package (8.5 ounces) cornbread mix

9 eggs, divided

¾ cup milk

8 ORTEGA® Taco Shells, any variety, crushed

1 tablespoon vegetable oil

1 onion, diced

1 red bell pepper, diced

1 pound lean ground beef

¾ cup water

1 packet (1.25 ounces) ORTEGA® Taco Seasoning Mix or 40% Less Sodium Taco Seasoning Mix

1 can (15 ounces) ORTEGA® Black Beans, rinsed, drained

1 cup ORTEGA® Thick & Chunky Salsa, any variety

1 can (4 ounces) ORTEGA® Fire-Roasted Diced Green Chiles

1 cup (4 ounces) shredded Cheddar cheese

COMBINE cornbread mix, 1 egg, milk and taco shells; mix well. Set aside.

HEAT oil in large cast-iron skillet over medium heat until hot. Add onion and bell pepper; cook and stir 3 to 4 minutes or until onion is translucent. Add ground beef; cook and stir until browned. Drain and discard fat.

ADD water and seasoning mix to skillet; mix well. Stir in beans and salsa; simmer 10 minutes, stirring occasionally.

BEAT remaining 8 eggs lightly; stir in chiles. Pour mixture into skillet. Spread prepared cornbread batter evenly over mixture with rubber spatula. Cover; cook over low heat 15 minutes or until toothpick inserted into center of cornbread comes out clean.

REMOVE lid; sprinkle evenly with cheese. Cover; cook over low heat 3 minutes or until cheese melts. Let stand 10 minutes before cutting into wedges to serve.

TIP

For an attractive presentation, bring the pie in the cast-iron skillet right to the table.

MEXED-UP FRENCH TOAST WITH SPICED CHOCOLATE DRIZZLE

MAKES 4 SERVINGS | PREP TIME 10 MINUTES **START TO FINISH** 20 MINUTES

6 eggs, beaten

½ cup half-and-half or milk

1 packet (1.25 ounces) ORTEGA® Taco Seasoning Mix or 40% Less Sodium Taco Seasoning Mix, divided

8 slices Texas toast-style bread, thawed if frozen

2 tablespoons butter

1 cup semisweet chocolate chips

¼ cup whipping cream

Maple Grove Farms® maple syrup

COMBINE eggs, half-and-half and 2 tablespoons seasoning mix in shallow bowl or pie pan; mix well.

PLACE bread slices in egg mixture, allowing bread to absorb mixture before turning to coat other side.

HEAT about ½ tablespoon butter in large skillet over medium heat. Place 2 egg-coated bread slices in skillet; cook about 4 minutes or until golden brown. Turn slices over and cook 4 minutes or until golden brown. Transfer to serving plate. Repeat with remaining butter and bread slices.

PLACE chocolate chips and remaining seasoning mix in small microwavable bowl. Microwave on HIGH 30 seconds; stir. Repeat as necessary until chips are melted and mixture is smooth. Stir in cream; mix well.

DRIZZLE chocolate mixture over French toast and serve with maple syrup.

TIP

If you can't find Texas toast in the bread section or freezer case, you can use day-old thick-cut white sandwich bread to make your own Texas toast.

BREAKFAST PANCAKE TACOS

MAKES 12 TACOS | PREP TIME 10 MINUTES **START TO FINISH** 15 MINUTES

1 can (16 ounces) ORTEGA®
Refried Beans

1 tablespoon butter

6 eggs, lightly beaten

1 can (4 ounces) ORTEGA®
Fire-Roasted Diced Green
Chiles

1 package (12-count) frozen
prepared pancakes

1 to 1½ cups cup ORTEGA® Salsa,
any variety

½ cup (2 ounces) shredded
Cheddar cheese

HEAT beans in small saucepan over medium-low heat, stirring occasionally.

MELT butter in medium skillet over medium heat. Add eggs; cook 2 to 3 minutes or just until set, lifting and stirring to scramble. Add chiles; mix well. Remove from heat; keep warm.

WRAP 4 pancakes in clean dish towel or paper towel; microwave on HIGH 30 seconds or until defrosted and warmed through. Repeat with remaining pancakes.

SPREAD beans evenly on pancakes; top evenly with scrambled eggs. Add salsa and cheese; fold in half to serve.

TIP

To make a delicious appetizer or brunch dish,
use smaller silver-dollar sized pancakes.

NEVER ENOUGH TACOS

TOMATILLO PORK TACOS

MAKES 4 SERVINGS (2 TACOS PER SERVING)

2 teaspoons canola oil

1 pound pork tenderloin, cut into ½-inch chunks

1 teaspoon ground cumin

1 teaspoon chili powder

½ cup chopped onion

3 cloves garlic, minced (optional)

¾ cup tomatillo salsa, divided

8 (6-inch) tortillas

1 cup diced ripe tomato

1 cup shredded romaine lettuce

½ cup (2 ounces) shredded 2% milk Mexican cheese blend or crumbled queso fresco cheese

1 Heat oil in large nonstick skillet over medium heat. Add pork, cumin and chili powder; stir until pork is coated with spices. Add onion and garlic, if desired; cook and stir 5 minutes or until pork is no longer pink. Add ½ cup salsa; simmer about 4 minutes or until pork is cooked through.

2 Wrap tortillas loosely in waxed paper and heat in microwave oven at MEDIUM (50%) 30 seconds or until warmed.

3 Serve pork mixture in tortillas topped with tomato, lettuce, cheese and remaining salsa.

CHIPOTLE TACO FILLING

MAKES 8 CUPS FILLING

- 2 pounds lean ground beef
- 2 cans (about 15 ounces each) pinto beans, rinsed and drained
- 2 cups chopped onions
- 1 can (about 14 ounces) diced tomatoes with peppers and onions, drained
- 2 chipotle peppers in adobo sauce, mashed
- 1 tablespoon beef bouillon granules
- 1 tablespoon sugar
- 1½ teaspoons ground cumin
- Taco shells or flour tortillas
- Shredded lettuce, salsa, shredded Mexican blend cheese and sour cream (optional)

SLOW COOKER DIRECTIONS

1 Brown beef in large nonstick skillet over medium-high heat 6 to 8 minutes, stirring to break up meat. Drain fat.

2 Combine beef, beans, onions, tomatoes, peppers, bouillon, sugar and cumin in 3½- to 4-quart slow cooker. Cover; cook on LOW 4 hours or on HIGH 2 hours.

3 Serve filling in taco shells. Top with lettuce, salsa, cheese and sour cream, if desired.

DOUBLE DUTY TACOS

MAKES 8 SERVINGS

MEXICALI CHILI RUB

¼ cup chili powder

3 tablespoons garlic salt

2 tablespoons ground cumin

2 tablespoons dried oregano

½ teaspoon ground red pepper

TACOS

2 pounds 90% lean ground beef

1 large onion, chopped

3 tablespoons Mexicali Chili Rub

¾ cup water

2 tablespoons tomato paste

16 packaged crispy taco shells

2 cups (8 ounces) shredded Monterey Jack or taco-flavored cheese

2 cups shredded lettuce

1 cup chopped tomatoes

1 cup diced ripe avocado

½ cup light or regular sour cream

Salsa

1 For rub, combine chili powder, garlic salt, cumin, oregano and ground red pepper in small bowl; mix well. Transfer to container with tight-fitting lid. Store in cool dry place up to 2 months.

2 Brown beef and onion in large deep skillet over medium-high heat, stirring to separate meat. Drain and discard fat. Sprinkle chili rub over beef mixture; cook 1 minute. Reduce heat to medium. Add water and tomato paste. Cover; simmer 5 minutes.

3 Spoon beef mixture into taco shells; top with cheese. Arrange lettuce, tomatoes, avocado, sour cream and salsa in bowls. Serve tacos with toppings as desired.

SERVING SUGGESTION

Serve with refried beans or Spanish rice.

CHICKEN AND SPICY BLACK BEAN TACOS

MAKES 4 SERVINGS

1 can (about 15 ounces) black beans, rinsed and drained

1 can (10 ounces) diced tomatoes with green chiles, drained

1½ teaspoons chili powder

¾ teaspoon ground cumin

1 tablespoon plus 1 teaspoon extra virgin olive oil, divided

12 ounces boneless skinless chicken breasts

12 crisp corn taco shells

Optional toppings: shredded lettuce, diced fresh tomatoes, shredded cheese, sour cream, sliced black olives

SLOW COOKER DIRECTIONS

1 Coat slow cooker with nonstick cooking spray. Add beans and tomatoes with chiles. Blend chili powder, cumin and 1 teaspoon oil in small bowl; rub onto chicken. Place chicken in slow cooker. Cover; cook on HIGH 1¾ hours.

2 Remove chicken and slice. Transfer bean mixture to bowl using slotted spoon. Stir in remaining 1 tablespoon oil.

3 To serve, warm taco shells according to package directions. Fill with equal amounts of bean mixture and chicken. Add toppings as desired.

TURKEY AND WINTER SQUASH TACOS

MAKES 2 SERVINGS

4 crisp corn taco shells

2 teaspoons vegetable oil

¼ cup finely chopped onion

1 cup diced cooked butternut or delicata squash

1 teaspoon taco seasoning mix

1 cup chopped cooked turkey, warmed

Salt and black pepper

¼ cup salsa

1 avocado, peeled and cut into 8 thin wedges

1 Preheat oven to 325°F. Place taco shells on baking sheet; heat according to package directions.

2 Meanwhile, heat oil in large skillet over medium-high heat. Add onion; cook and stir 3 minutes. Add squash and seasoning mix; cook and stir 2 to 3 minutes.

3 To assemble tacos, place ¼ cup turkey in each taco shell. Season with salt and pepper. Top with squash mixture, 1 tablespoon salsa and 2 slices avocado.

NOTE

Some supermarkets carry packaged diced squash; simply follow the cooking instructions on the package. To use whole squash, peel the squash, cut in half and remove the seeds. Cut the squash into ¾-inch-long strips, then cut crosswise into ¾-inch chunks. Measure 1 cup squash. Heat 1 tablespoon vegetable oil in a medium skillet over medium-low heat. Add the squash; cook and stir 10 to 15 minutes or until fork-tender.

FISH TACOS WITH YOGURT SAUCE

MAKES 6 SERVINGS

SAUCE

- ½ cup plain yogurt
- ¼ cup chopped fresh cilantro
- 3 tablespoons sour cream
- Juice of 1 lime
- 1 tablespoon mayonnaise
- ½ teaspoon ground cumin
- ¼ teaspoon ground red pepper
- Salt and black pepper

TACOS

- Juice of ½ lime
- 2 tablespoons canola oil
- 1½ pounds swordfish, halibut or tilapia fillets
- Salt and ground black pepper
- 12 corn or flour tortillas
- 3 cups shredded cabbage or prepared coleslaw mixture
- 2 medium tomatoes, chopped

1 For sauce, mix yogurt, cilantro, sour cream, lime juice, mayonnaise, cumin and red pepper in small bowl. Season with salt and black pepper to taste.

2 For tacos, preheat grill or broiler. Combine juice of ½ lime and oil in small bowl. Brush or spoon lime and oil mixture over fish fillets about 5 minutes before cooking. Season with salt and black pepper. (Do not marinate fish longer than about 5 minutes, or acid in lime will begin to "cook" fish.)

3 If grilling fish, spray grid or grill basket with nonstick cooking spray. Prepare grill for direct cooking. Place fish on grid over high heat. Grill, covered 10 minutes, turning once. If broiling fish, spray broiler pan with nonstick cooking spray. Broil 4 inches from heat about 5 minutes; turn and broil 5 minutes more or until center is opaque. Remove from broiler. Flake fish or break into large pieces.

4 Place tortillas on grill or on burner over medium heat. Grill 10 seconds on each side or until beginning to bubble and brown lightly. Fill tortillas with fish. Top with sauce, cabbage and tomatoes.

SOUTHWEST BUFFALO CHICKEN TACOS

MAKES 4 SERVINGS | PREP TIME 5 MINUTES **START TO FINISH** 10 MINUTES

3 tablespoons ORTEGA® Taco Sauce, any variety

½ teaspoon cornstarch

7 ounces chunk chicken breast

4 ORTEGA® Whole Grain Corn Taco Shells

1 stalk celery, diced

½ cup crumbled blue cheese

COMBINE taco sauce and cornstarch in small bowl; mix well.

HEAT small skillet over medium heat. Add chicken and taco sauce mixture; stir well. Reduce heat; cook and stir 4 minutes or until mixture has thickened.

DIVIDE filling evenly among taco shells. Top evenly with celery and blue cheese.

NEVER ENOUGH TACOS

SIMPLE SHREDDED PORK TACOS

MAKES 6 SERVINGS

2 pounds boneless pork roast

1 cup salsa

1 can (4 ounces) diced mild green chiles, drained

½ teaspoon garlic salt

½ teaspoon black pepper

Flour or corn tortillas, warmed

SLOW COOKER DIRECTIONS

1 Place all ingredients, except tortillas, in slow cooker.

2 Cover; cook on LOW 8 hours or until meat is tender. Shred pork; serve on warmed tortillas.

NEVER ENOUGH TACOS

SPICY BEEF TACOS

MAKES 6 SERVINGS

1 pound boneless beef chuck, cut into 1-inch cubes

Vegetable oil

1 to 2 teaspoons chili powder

1 clove garlic, minced

½ teaspoon salt

½ teaspoon ground cumin

1 can (about 14 ounces) diced tomatoes

12 (6-inch) corn tortillas*

1 cup (4 ounces) shredded mild Cheddar cheese

2 to 3 cups shredded iceberg lettuce

1 large fresh tomato, seeded and chopped

Chopped fresh cilantro (optional)

Or, substitute packaged taco shells for the corn tortillas. Omit steps 4 and 5. Warm taco shells according to package directions.

1 Brown beef in 2 tablespoons hot oil in large skillet over medium-high heat 10 to 12 minutes, turning frequently. Reduce heat to low. Stir in chili powder, garlic, salt and cumin. Cook and stir 30 seconds.

2 Add diced tomatoes with juice. Bring to a boil over high heat. Reduce heat to low. Cover and simmer 1½ to 2 hours until beef is very tender.

3 Using two forks, pull beef into coarse shreds in skillet. Increase heat to medium. Cook, uncovered, 10 to 15 minutes until most of liquid has evaporated. Keep warm.

4 Heat 4 to 5 inches of oil in deep fat fryer or deep saucepan over medium-high heat to 375°F; adjust heat to maintain temperature.

5 For taco shells, place 1 tortilla in taco fryer basket;** close gently. Fry tortilla 30 seconds to 1 minute until crisp and golden. Open basket; gently remove taco shell. Drain on paper towels. Repeat with remaining tortillas.

6 Layer beef, cheese, lettuce and tomato in each taco shell. Garnish with cilantro, if desired.

**Taco fryer baskets are available in large supermarkets and housewares stores.

FISH TACOS WITH CILANTRO CREAM SAUCE

MAKES 4 SERVINGS (2 TACOS PER SERVING)

½ cup sour cream

¼ cup chopped fresh cilantro

1¼ teaspoons ground cumin, divided

1 pound skinless tilapia, mahimahi or other firm white fish fillets

1 teaspoon chipotle hot pepper sauce, divided

1 teaspoon garlic salt

2 teaspoons canola or vegetable oil

1 red bell pepper, cut into strips

1 green bell pepper, cut into strips

8 corn tortillas, warmed

4 limes, cut into wedges

1 For Cilantro Cream Sauce, combine sour cream, cilantro and ¼ teaspoon cumin in small bowl. Refrigerate until needed.

2 Cut fish into 1-inch chunks; toss with ½ teaspoon hot pepper sauce, remaining 1 teaspoon cumin and garlic salt in medium bowl. Heat oil in large nonstick skillet over medium heat. Add fish; cook, turning gently, 3 to 4 minutes or until fish is opaque in center. Transfer to plate.

3 Add bell peppers to skillet; stir-fry 6 to 8 minutes or until tender. Return fish to skillet, adding remaining ½ teaspoon hot pepper sauce; toss with bell peppers and cook just until heated through.

4 Spoon mixture into warm tortillas. Serve with Cilantro Cream Sauce and lime wedges.

TURKEY TACOS

MAKES 4 SERVINGS (2 TACOS PER SERVING)

1 pound raw turkey breast cutlets,* sliced ¼-inch thick

Juice of 1 lime

¼ teaspoon chipotle chili powder

1 jalapeño pepper,** cored, seeded and minced

1 can (about 15 ounces) pinto beans, rinsed and drained

¼ teaspoon salt

¼ teaspoon ground cumin

8 corn taco shells

½ cup finely chopped romaine lettuce

1 small onion, chopped

¼ cup minced fresh cilantro

¼ cup salsa, drained of excess liquid

Or, you can substitute with boneless skinless chicken breasts, sliced to ¼-inch thickness.

**Jalapeño peppers can sting and irritate the skin, so wear rubber gloves when handling peppers and do not touch your eyes.*

1 Place turkey in shallow glass bowl. Add lime juice and chile powder. Turn to coat turkey. Set aside at room temperature 15 minutes. Coat small skillet with nonstick cooking spray and heat over medium heat. Add jalapeño pepper and cook 1 to 2 minutes to soften. Add beans, salt and cumin; heat through. Set aside.

2 Preheat grill to medium-high heat. Spray grid with cooking spray. Grill turkey about 2 minutes per side or until cooked through. Cut into bite-size strips.

3 Heat taco shells, if desired. Divide turkey strips among taco shells. Top each taco with about 1 tablespoon of beans. Sprinkle with lettuce, onion, cilantro and salsa. Serve immediately.

CITRUS CRAB TACOS WITH APRICOT COCKTAIL SAUCE

MAKES 6 SERVINGS

1 can lump crabmeat (cooked)

1 lemon, juiced

1 lime, juiced

1 tablespoon chopped cilantro

2 plum tomatoes, finely chopped

1 tablespoon seafood seasoning

Salt and black pepper, to taste

1 cup **HEINZ**® Original Cocktail Sauce

3 tablespoons apricot preserves

12 small flour tortillas

1 bunch baby arugula

1 pint alfalfa sprouts

1 In a medium mixing bowl, add crabmeat, lemon and lime juice, chopped cilantro, tomatoes and seafood seasoning, and mix well. Season with salt and pepper to taste and place in fridge until ready to serve.

2 In a food processor, add Cocktail Sauce and apricot preserves and blend until thoroughly mixed.

3 When ready to serve, assemble tacos by adding crabmeat, a pinch of baby arugula and sprouts, then top with apricot cocktail sauce. Fasten taco together with toothpicks.

4 Serve cold.

TIP

The apricot cocktail sauce also makes an excellent spread for sandwiches and can be used as a dipping sauce.

SOFT TURKEY TACOS

MAKES 4 SERVINGS

8 (6-inch) corn tortillas*

1½ teaspoons vegetable oil

1 pound ground turkey

1 small onion, chopped

1 teaspoon dried oregano

Salt and black pepper

Chopped tomatoes

Shredded lettuce

Salsa

Refried beans (optional)

*Substitute 8 (10-inch) flour
tortillas for corn tortillas, if desired.

1 Wrap tortillas in foil. Place in cold oven; set temperature to 350°F.

2 Heat oil in large skillet over medium heat. Add turkey and onion; cook until turkey is no longer pink, stirring occasionally. Stir in oregano. Season with salt and pepper to taste. Keep warm.

3 For each taco, fill warm tortilla with turkey mixture; top with tomatoes, lettuce and salsa. Serve with refried beans, if desired.

NOTE

To warm tortillas in microwave oven, wrap loosely in damp paper towel. Microwave on HIGH 2 minutes or until hot.

TERRIFIC TACOS

MAKES 24 TACOS | PREP TIME 15 MINUTES **COOK TIME** 15 MINUTES

2 pounds ground beef

1 jar (16 ounces) PACE® Picante Sauce

24 taco shells

Shredded Cheddar cheese

Shredded lettuce

Chopped tomato

Sour cream

1 In a 12-inch skillet over medium-high heat, cook ground beef until browned, stirring to separate the meat. Pour off any fat. Add picante sauce. Heat to a boil. Simmer 5 minutes.

2 Spoon taco mixture into taco shells. Top with cheese, lettuce, tomatoes and sour cream.

RAMEN "SPAGHETTI" TACOS

MAKES 4 SERVINGS

2 packages (3 ounces each) ramen noodles, any flavor*

1 cup pasta sauce

8 hard taco shells

½ cup grated mozzarella cheese

¼ cup (2 ounces) shredded Cheddar cheese

Chopped tomatoes

Discard seasoning packets.

1 Cook noodles according to package directions. Drain; return to saucepan. Add pasta sauce. Cook over medium heat until heated through.

2 Divide noodles evenly among taco shells. Top each taco with mozzarella and Cheddar cheeses. Microwave on HIGH at 10- to 15-second intervals until cheeses are melted, if desired. Top with tomatoes.

TIP

These tacos can be flavored in a variety of ways. Try them with salsa instead of pasta sauce and toppings such as sour cream, guacamole, shredded lettuce and grated Mexican cheese. Or, mix cooked noodles with teriyaki sauce and top with shredded cabbage, water chestnuts, bamboo shoots and chicken or pork.

REDHOT TACOS

MAKES 4 SERVINGS | PREP TIME 5 MINUTES **COOK TIME** 10 MINUTES

1 pound ground beef or turkey

1 cup salsa

¼ cup FRANK'S® RedHot® Original Cayenne Pepper Sauce

2 teaspoons chili powder

8 taco shells, heated

Garnish: chopped tomatoes, shredded lettuce, sliced olives, sour cream, shredded cheese

COOK beef in skillet over medium-high heat 5 minutes or until browned, stirring to separate meat; drain. Stir in salsa, **FRANK'S RedHot** Sauce and chili powder. Heat to boiling. Reduce heat to medium-low. Cook 5 minutes, stirring often.

TO SERVE, spoon meat mixture into taco shells. Splash on more **FRANK'S RedHot** Sauce to taste. Garnish as desired with taco toppings.

TIP

For tacos that don't break, fill shells with meat mixture, then microwave 4 tacos at a time for 1 to 2 minutes until warm.

SPEEDY TACOS

MAKES 2 SERVINGS (3 TACOS EACH)

4 ounces ground beef sirloin

¼ cup chopped onion

1 clove garlic, minced

⅓ cup tomato sauce

1 tablespoon taco seasoning mix

6 taco shells

¼ cup (2 ounces) shredded Cheddar cheese

½ cup shredded lettuce

⅓ cup chopped tomato

¼ cup chopped onion

Hot pepper sauce (optional)

1 Heat small skillet over medium heat until hot. Add beef, onion and garlic; cook and stir 5 minutes until beef is browned, breaking up meat with spoon. Add tomato sauce and seasoning mix; cook 5 minutes.

2 Warm taco shells in oven following package directions.

3 Fill taco shells with meat mixture, cheese, lettuce, tomato and onion. Serve with hot pepper sauce, if desired.

SOFT TACOS WITH CHICKEN

MAKES 8 TACOS

8 (6- or 7-inch) corn tortillas

2 tablespoons butter or margarine

1 medium onion, chopped

1½ cups shredded cooked chicken

1 can (4 ounces) diced mild green chiles, drained

2 tablespoons chopped fresh cilantro

1 cup (½ pint) sour cream

Salt

Black pepper

1½ cups (6 ounces) shredded Monterey Jack cheese

1 large avocado, diced

Green taco sauce

1 Stack and wrap tortillas in foil. Warm in 350°F oven 15 minutes or until heated through.

2 Melt butter in large skillet over medium heat. Add onion; cook until tender. Add chicken, chiles and cilantro. Cook 3 minutes or until mixture is hot. Reduce heat to low. Stir in sour cream; season with salt and pepper. Heat gently; do not boil.

3 To assemble tacos, spoon about 3 tablespoons chicken mixture into center of each tortilla; sprinkle with 2 tablespoons cheese. Top with avocado; drizzle with 1 to 2 teaspoons taco sauce. Sprinkle tacos with remaining cheese. Roll tortilla into cone shape or fold in half to eat.

FISH TACOS WITH
CITRUS PINEAPPLE SALSA

MAKES 4 SERVINGS | PREP TIME 10 MINUTES **COOK TIME** 10 MINUTES

2 cups shredded red cabbage

1 jar (16 ounces) PACE® Citrus
  Pineapple Salsa

1¼ pounds cod **or** tilapia

1 teaspoon ground cumin

1 tablespoon olive oil

8 flour tortillas **or** corn tortillas
  (6-inch), warmed

1 cup cotija cheese **or** feta cheese

¼ cup chopped fresh cilantro

1 Stir the cabbage and ½ **cup** salsa in a medium bowl. Season the fish with the cumin.

2 Heat the oil in a 12-inch skillet over medium-high heat. Add the fish and cook for 3 minutes per side or until the fish flakes easily when tested with a fork. Add ½ **cup** salsa. Break the fish pieces up with a fork and stir to coat.

3 Spoon about ⅓ **cup** fish mixture into each tortilla. Top **each** with **about ¼ cup** cabbage mixture and **2 tablespoons** cheese. Top with the remaining salsa. Sprinkle with the cilantro and fold the tortillas around the filling.

BEER-BRAISED SPICY BEEF TACOS

MAKES 6 SERVINGS

1 beef Shoulder Center Roast
  (2 pounds)

2 teaspoons olive oil

Salt and pepper

1 bottle (12 ounces) beer

2 medium chipotle peppers in
  adobo sauce, minced

2 tablespoons plus 1 teaspoon
  adobo sauce from chipotle
  peppers, divided

12 small corn or flour tortillas
  (6-inch diameter), warmed

2 cups coleslaw

TOPPINGS

Chopped red onion, chopped
fresh cilantro, crumbled queso
or sour cream, fresh lime juice
or lime wedges (optional)

1 Heat oil in stockpot over medium heat until hot. Place beef roast in stockpot, brown evenly. Pour off drippings; season with salt and pepper, as desired.

2 Add beer, peppers and 2 tablespoons adobo sauce to stockpot; bring to a boil. Reduce heat; cover tightly and simmer 2¼ to 2½ hours or until pot roast is fork-tender.

3 Meanwhile, combine coleslaw and remaining 1 teaspoon adobo sauce. Refrigerate until ready to use.

4 Remove roast, cool slightly. Skim fat from cooking liquid; bring to boil. Reduce to medium and cook 10 to 12 minutes or until reduced to 1½ cups. Meanwhile, trim and discard excess fat from cooked roast. Shred roast with 2 forks. Return beef to reserved liquid; cook over medium heat until heated through.

5 Serve beef in tortillas; top with coleslaw mixture and toppings, as desired.

COOK'S TIP

Two pounds beef Shoulder Roast Boneless may be substituted.

courtesy The Beef Checkoff

SPIRALED SWEET POTATO AND BLACK BEAN TACOS

MAKES 4 SERVINGS

¼ cup sour cream

2 tablespoons mayonnaise

Juice of 1 lime

½ teaspoon chipotle chili powder

1 can (about 15 ounces) black beans, undrained

1 teaspoon smoked paprika

1 sweet potato, peeled

1 red onion

1 green bell pepper

4 teaspoons vegetable oil, divided

¼ teaspoon salt

8 small taco-size tortillas

1 avocado, sliced

¼ cup chopped fresh cilantro

¼ cup grated or shredded cojita cheese

1 Combine sour cream, mayonnaise, lime juice and chili powder in small bowl; mix well. Refrigerate until ready to use. Combine beans with liquid and paprika in small saucepan. Cook over medium-low heat 5 to 7 minutes or until heated through, stirring occasionally. Remove from heat; coarsely mash beans with potato masher, leaving some beans whole. Keep warm.

2 Spiral* sweet potato with medium spiral blade; cut into desired lengths. Spiral* onion with fine spiral blade and bell pepper with spiral slicing blade; cut into desired lengths.

3 Heat 2 teaspoons oil in medium nonstick skillet over medium heat. Add sweet potato; cook and stir 7 to 10 minutes or until tender. Sprinkle with salt.

4 Heat remaining 2 teaspoons oil in large nonstick skillet over high heat. Add onion and bell pepper; cook and stir 5 minutes or until vegetables are browned and softened.

5 Spread beans down middle of tortillas. Top with sweet potatoes, vegetables, sour cream mixture, avocado, cilantro and cheese; fold in half.

If you don't have a spiral cutter, you can slice or chop the vegetables.

BRAISED BRISKET STREET-STYLE TACOS

MAKES 8 TO 10 SERVINGS

1 beef Brisket Flat Half (3 to 3½ pounds)

1 tablespoon olive oil

½ teaspoon salt

¼ teaspoon pepper

1 large onion, sliced

4 cloves garlic, minced

1 bottle (12 ounces) beer

1¼ cups tomatillo salsa, divided

16 to 20 small corn tortillas (about 6-inch diameter), warmed

TOPPINGS

Chopped fresh tomatoes, chopped onion, chopped fresh cilantro or prepared pico de gallo (optional)

1 Heat oil in stockpot over medium heat until hot. Place beef Brisket in stockpot; brown evenly. Remove Brisket; season with salt and pepper.

2 Add onion and garlic to stockpot; cook and stir 4 to 5 minutes or until onion is crisp-tender. Return Brisket, fat-side up, to stockpot. Add beer and 1 cup salsa; bring to a boil. Reduce heat; cover tightly and simmer 2½ to 3 hours or until Brisket is fork-tender.

3 Remove Brisket; keep warm. Skim fat from cooking liquid; bring to a boil. Cook 18 to 20 minutes or until reduced by half. Stir in remaining ¼ cup salsa. Meanwhile, trim fat from brisket. Carve diagonally across the grain into thin slices. Return beef to cooking liquid and heat through. Serve beef in tortillas. Garnish with Toppings, as desired.

courtesy The Beef Checkoff

DEVIL'S FIRE SHREDDED BEEF TACOS

MAKES 6 TO 8 SERVINGS

1 boneless beef chuck roast (2½ pounds)

1¼ teaspoons salt, divided

1 teaspoon *each* cumin, garlic powder and smoked paprika

2 tablespoons olive oil, divided

2 cups beef broth

1 red bell pepper, sliced

1 tomato, cut into wedges

½ onion, sliced

2 cloves garlic, minced

1 to 2 canned chipotle peppers in adobo sauce

Juice of 1 lime

Corn or flour tortillas

OPTIONAL TOPPINGS

Sliced bell peppers, avocado, diced onion, lime wedges and or chopped fresh cilantro

1 Season beef with 1 teaspoon salt, cumin, garlic powder and smoked paprika. Heat 1 tablespoon oil in large skillet over medium-high heat. Add beef; cook 5 minutes on each side until browned. Remove to slow cooker.

2 Pour in broth. Cover; cook on LOW 8 to 9 hours or on HIGH 4 to 5 hours.

3 Meanwhile, preheat oven to 425°F. Combine bell pepper, tomato, onion and garlic on large baking sheet. Drizzle with remaining 1 tablespoon oil. Roast 40 minutes or until vegetables are tender. Place vegetables, chipotle pepper, lime juice and remaining ¼ teaspoon salt in food processor or blender; blend until smooth.

4 Remove beef to large cutting board; shred with two forks. Combine shredded meat with 1 cup cooking liquid. Discard remaining cooking liquid. Serve on tortillas with sauce. Top as desired.

DINNER WINNERS

CHILI IN TORTILLA BOWLS

MAKES 6 SERVINGS | PREP TIME 10 MINUTES **COOK TIME** 25 MINUTES

1½ pounds ground turkey

1 medium onion, chopped

1 large red bell pepper, diced

2 tablespoons chili powder

1 can (19 ounces) red kidney
    beans, rinsed and drained

1 can (11 ounces) whole kernel
    corn, drained

1 jar (1 pound 8 ounces) RAGÚ®
    Chunky Pasta Sauce

6 burrito-size whole wheat,
    spinach or tomato tortillas

1 cup shredded 2% cheddar
    cheese (about 4 ounces)

1 In 12-inch skillet, brown ground turkey over medium-high heat, stirring
   occasionally. Add onion, red pepper and chili powder and cook, stirring
   occasionally, 5 minutes or until onion is tender. Stir in beans, corn and
   Pasta Sauce.

2 Bring to a boil over high heat. Reduce heat to low and simmer covered, stirring
   occasionally, 20 minutes.

3 Meanwhile, using one tortilla at a time, press into a 1- or 2-cup microwave-safe
   bowl to form bowl shape. Microwave at HIGH 1½ minutes. Let cool 1 minute.
   Gently lift out and arrange on serving plate. Repeat with remaining tortillas.

4 To serve, spoon chili into tortilla bowls, then sprinkle with cheese.

SPICY BURRITO BURGERS

MAKES 4 SERVINGS

6 tablespoons mild salsa, divided

1 can (about 4 ounces) diced green chiles, divided

¼ cup sour cream

Dash hot pepper sauce

1 pound ground beef

4 (8-inch) flour tortillas

1 cup shredded lettuce

½ cup (2 ounces) shredded taco-flavored Cheddar cheese

1 Prepare grill for direct cooking. Combine 2 tablespoons salsa, 2 tablespoons chiles, sour cream and hot pepper sauce in small bowl; set aside.

2 Combine beef, remaining 4 tablespoons salsa and remaining chiles in large bowl; mix well. Shape into four 4-inch oval patties.

3 Grill over medium heat, covered, 8 to 10 minutes (or uncovered, 13 to 15 minutes) or until cooked through (160°F), turning once.

4 Place one burger in center of one tortilla. Top each with one quarter of lettuce, cheese and sour cream mixture. Bring edges of tortillas together over top of burgers; secure with toothpicks if necessary. Remove toothpicks before serving.

MEXICAN CASSEROLE WITH TORTILLA CHIPS

MAKES 4 SERVINGS

12 ounces lean ground turkey

1 can (about 14 ounces) stewed tomatoes

½ of a 16-ounce package frozen bell pepper stir-fry blend, thawed

¾ teaspoon ground cumin

½ teaspoon salt (optional)

1½ ounces finely shredded sharp Cheddar cheese

2 ounces tortilla chips, lightly crushed

1 Spray large nonstick skillet with nonstick cooking spray. Cook turkey over medium heat until no longer pink, stirring to break up meat. Stir in tomatoes, bell peppers and cumin; bring to a boil. Reduce heat; cover and simmer 20 minutes or until vegetables are tender.

2 Stir in salt, if desired. Sprinkle evenly with cheese and chips.

VARIATION

Sprinkle chips into a casserole. Spread cooked turkey mixture evenly over the chips and top with cheese.

EASY TACO SALAD

MAKES 6 SERVINGS | PREP TIME 10 MINUTES **START TO FINISH** 15 MINUTES

1 pound lean ground beef

¾ cup water

1 ORTEGA® Taco Dinner Kit—
includes 12 taco shells,
1 packet (1.25 ounces) taco
seasoning mix and 1 packet
(3 ounces) taco sauce

2 cups torn lettuce

1 cup chopped red onion

1 cup (4 ounces) shredded
Cheddar cheese

1 cup chopped tomato

1 can (2.25 ounces) B&G® Sliced
Ripe Olives, drained

½ cup sour cream

Additional ORTEGA® Taco Sauce,
any variety (optional)

BROWN and stir beef in medium skillet over medium-high heat until no longer pink. Drain and discard fat. Stir in water and taco seasoning mix from Taco Kit; bring to a boil. Reduce heat to low. Cook and stir 5 to 6 minutes or until thickened.

BREAK taco shells from Taco Kit into bite-size pieces. Combine beef mixture with taco shells, lettuce, onion, cheese, tomato and olives; toss well.

COMBINE sour cream and taco sauce from Taco Kit in small bowl; mix well. Serve as dressing with salad. Top salad with additional taco sauce, if desired.

TIP

You can make this salad to take along to a potluck or a picnic.
For best results, blend in the taco shell pieces just before serving.

CHORIZO AND PAPA BURRITOS

MAKES 8 MINI BURRITOS

14 ounces chorizo sausage

2 small russet potatoes, peeled and diced (about 6 ounces)

8 taco-size flour tortillas

½ cup (2 ounces) shredded Monterey Jack cheese

¼ cup sour cream

1 Remove and discard casing from chorizo. Heat medium skillet over medium heat until hot. Crumble chorizo into skillet; brown 6 to 8 minutes, stirring to separate meat. When chorizo begins to release fat, add potatoes. Cook about 12 minutes or until potatoes are tender, stirring frequently. Drain excess fat.

2 Heat tortillas: On a gas stove, place tortilla directly onto burner over low flame; turn with tongs when tortilla begins to brown, about 10 seconds. Heat until browned on both sides. On electric range, preheat burner 2 minutes on medium heat. Place tortilla directly onto burner; turn with tongs when tortilla begins to brown, about 10 seconds. Heat until browned on both sides.

3 Spoon about ¼ cup chorizo mixture in center of each tortilla; top with 1 tablespoon cheese and 1½ teaspoons sour cream. Fold right side of tortilla over mixture. Fold bottom of tortillas up over bottom third of filling. Fold in sides of tortillas over filling.

NOTE

If using 4 fajita-size flour tortillas, use ½ cup filling per tortilla.

CHEESY CHICKEN CHILI

MAKES 4 SERVINGS | PREP TIME 10 MINUTES **COOK TIME** 20 MINUTES

1½ Tbsp. olive or vegetable oil

1 lb. boneless, skinless chicken breast halves, cut into ¾-inch chunks

2 Tbsp. ground cumin

1 jar (16 oz.) salsa

2 cans (16 oz. each) great northern beans, drained and rinsed

1 cup frozen corn

1½ cups (6 oz.) SARGENTO® Fine Cut Shredded Colby-Jack Cheese or Sargento® Fine Cut Shredded Monterey Jack Cheese, divided

Sour cream, sliced green onions, sliced black olives and crushed tortilla chips (optional)

HEAT oil in large saucepan over medium heat. Add chicken; cook 3 minutes, stirring frequently. Add cumin; cook 1 minute, stir constantly. Add salsa, beans and corn; bring to a boil. Reduce heat; cover and simmer 15 minutes, stirring once.

REMOVE from heat; stir in 1 cup cheese. Ladle into bowls; top with remaining cheese and serve with sour cream, green onions, black olives and tortilla chips, as desired.

MEXICAN STUFFED PEPPERS

MAKES 4 SERVINGS

6 ounces breakfast bulk turkey sausage

1 cup frozen corn

4 ounces uncooked orzo pasta or small shell pasta

1 cup canned black beans, rinsed and drained

Salsa Cruda (recipe follows) or 1¾ cups mild picante sauce, divided

½ cup water

¼ cup cornmeal

1 tablespoon chili powder

½ teaspoon ground cumin

4 medium green bell peppers, halved lengthwise with stems and seeds removed

½ cup (2 ounces) shredded sharp Cheddar cheese

½ cup sour cream

¼ cup chopped fresh cilantro or finely chopped green onions

1 Preheat oven to 350°F. Spray large nonstick skillet with nonstick cooking spray. Heat over high heat until hot. Brown turkey over medium-high heat 6 to 8 minutes or until no longer pink, stirring to separate turkey; drain fat. Add corn, pasta, beans, 1¼ cups Salsa Cruda, water, cornmeal, chili powder and cumin. Bring to a boil; remove from heat.

2 Place pepper halves in 13×9-inch baking pan. Fill each pepper half with equal amounts of sausage mixture; cover tightly with foil. Bake 1 hour and 15 minutes. Remove from oven; top each pepper half with ⅛ remaining Salsa Cruda. Sprinkle cheese over peppers. Top each half with 1 tablespoon sour cream; sprinkle with cilantro.

SALSA CRUDA

2 cups chopped tomato

¼ cup minced onion

¼ cup minced fresh cilantro (optional)

¼ cup fresh lime juice

1 jalapeño pepper,* seeded, minced

2 cloves garlic, minced

*Jalapeño peppers can sting and irritate the skin, so wear rubber gloves when handling peppers and do not touch your eyes.

Combine tomato, onion, cilantro, if desired, lime juice, jalapeño pepper and garlic in small bowl. Stir to combine.

MEXICAN TORTILLA STACK-UPS

MAKES 6 SERVINGS

1 tablespoon vegetable oil

½ cup chopped onion

1 can (about 15 ounces) black beans, rinsed and drained

1 can (about 14 ounces) Mexican- or Italian-style diced tomatoes

1 cup frozen corn

1 packet (1¼ ounces) taco seasoning mix

6 (6-inch) corn tortillas

2 cups (8 ounces) shredded Mexican cheese blend

1 cup water

Sour cream (optional)

Sliced black olives (optional)

1 Preheat oven to 350°F. Spray 13×9-inch baking dish with nonstick cooking spray.

2 Heat oil in large skillet over medium-high heat. Add onion; cook and stir 3 minutes or until tender. Add beans, tomatoes, corn and seasoning mix; bring to a boil over high heat. Reduce heat to low and simmer 5 minutes.

3 Place 2 tortillas side by side in prepared dish. Top each tortilla with about ½ cup bean mixture. Sprinkle evenly with one third of cheese. Repeat layers twice. Pour water around edges of tortillas.

4 Cover tightly with foil and bake 30 to 35 minutes or until heated through. Cut into wedges to serve. Serve with sour cream and black olives, if desired.

TACO TATER BITES

MAKES 6 SERVINGS | PREP TIME 10 MINUTES **START TO FINISH** 20 MINUTES

1 bag (16 ounces) frozen formed potato nuggets

1 tablespoon olive oil

1 small onion, chopped

1 pound ground beef

¾ cup water

1 can (4 ounces) ORTEGA® Diced Jalapeños

1 packet (1.25 ounces) ORTEGA® 40% Less Sodium Taco Seasoning Mix

1½ cups prepared queso sauce or cheese sauce

BAKE potato nuggets according to package instructions.

HEAT olive oil in medium skillet over medium heat. Add onions; cook and stir 3 minutes or until browned. Add beef; cook and stir 5 minutes or until no longer pink. Stir in water, jalapeños and seasoning mix. Remove from heat; let stand to thicken.

TOP potato nuggets with beef mixture and queso sauce to serve.

TIP

Boost the flavor of these bites by serving with additional ORTEGA® Diced Jalapeños. Or, garnish with ORTEGA® Fire-Roasted Diced Green Chiles and chopped white onions.

HEARTY CHICKEN CHILI

MAKES 6 SERVINGS

1 onion, finely chopped

1 jalapeño pepper,* minced

1 clove garlic, minced

1½ teaspoons chili powder

¾ teaspoon salt

½ teaspoon ground cumin

½ teaspoon dried oregano

½ teaspoon black pepper

¼ teaspoon red pepper flakes (optional)

1½ pounds boneless skinless chicken thighs, cut into 1-inch pieces

2 cans (about 15 ounces each) hominy, rinsed and drained

1 can (about 15 ounces) pinto beans, rinsed and drained

1 cup chicken broth

1 tablespoon all-purpose flour (optional)

Chopped fresh Italian parsley or cilantro (optional)

Jalapeño peppers can sting and irritate the skin, so wear rubber gloves when handling peppers and do not touch your eyes.

SLOW COOKER DIRECTIONS

1 Combine onion, jalapeño pepper, garlic, chili powder, salt, cumin, oregano, black pepper and red pepper flakes, if desired, in slow cooker.

2 Add chicken, hominy, beans and broth; stir well to combine. Cover; cook on LOW 7 hours.

3 For thicker chili, stir 1 tablespoon flour into 3 tablespoons cooking liquid in small bowl. Stir into slow cooker. *Turn slow cooker to HIGH.* Cover; cook 10 minutes or until thickened. Garnish with parsley.

MONTEREY CHICKEN TORTILLA CASSEROLE

MAKES 4 SERVINGS | PREP TIME 15 MINUTES **BAKE TIME** 40 MINUTES

1 cup coarsely crumbled tortilla chips

2 cups cubed cooked chicken **or** turkey

1 can (about 15 ounces) cream-style corn

¾ cup PACE® Picante Sauce

½ cup sliced pitted black olives

½ cup shredded Cheddar cheese (2 ounces)

¼ cup chopped green pepper

1 Layer the crumbled chips, chicken, corn and picante sauce in a 1-quart casserole. Top with the olives and cheese.

2 Bake at 350°F. for 40 minutes or until the mixture is hot and bubbling. Top with the pepper.

MEXICAN PIZZA

MAKES 8 SERVINGS

1 package (about 14 ounces) refrigerated pizza dough

1 cup chunky salsa

1 teaspoon ground cumin

1 cup canned black beans, rinsed and drained*

1 cup frozen corn, thawed

½ cup sliced green onions

1½ cups (6 ounces) shredded 2% Mexican cheese blend

½ cup chopped fresh cilantro (optional)

*Save the remaining ¾ cup beans (from a 15- or 16-ounce can) in the refrigerator for up to 4 days to add to salads or soups.

1 Preheat oven to 425°F. Unroll pizza dough onto 15×10×1-inch jelly-roll pan coated with nonstick cooking spray; press dough evenly to all edges of pan. Bake 8 minutes.

2 Combine salsa and cumin in small bowl; spread over partially baked crust. Top with beans, corn and green onions. Bake 8 minutes or until crust is deep golden brown. Top with cheese; continue baking 2 minutes or until cheese is melted. Cut into squares; garnish with cilantro, if desired.

CRUNCHY LAYERED BEEF & BEAN SALAD

MAKES 6 SERVINGS | PREP TIME 10 MINUTES **COOK TIME** 6 MINUTES

1 pound ground beef or turkey

2 cans (15 to 19 ounces each) black beans or pinto beans, rinsed and drained

1 can (14½ ounces) stewed tomatoes, undrained

1⅓ cups FRENCH'S® French Fried Onions, divided

1 tablespoon FRANK'S® RedHot® Original Cayenne Pepper Sauce

1 packet (1¼ ounces) taco seasoning mix

6 cups shredded lettuce

1 cup (4 ounces) shredded Cheddar or Monterey Jack cheese

COOK beef in large nonstick skillet over medium heat until thoroughly browned; drain well. Stir in beans, tomatoes, *⅔ cup* French Fried Onions, **FRANK'S RedHot** Sauce and seasoning mix. Heat to boiling. Cook over medium heat 5 minutes, stirring occasionally.

SPOON beef mixture over lettuce on serving platter. Top with cheese.

MICROWAVE remaining *⅔ cup* onions 1 minute on HIGH. Sprinkle over salad.

TACO STEW

MAKES 5 SERVINGS

½ pound 95% lean ground beef

1 cup chopped onion

1 can (16 ounces) pinto beans in Mexican-style sauce

1 can (about 14 ounces) stewed tomatoes, undrained

1 can (10 ounces) diced tomatoes with green chiles

2 teaspoons chili powder

5 (8-inch) corn tortillas

5 cups shredded iceberg lettuce

½ cup (2 ounces) shredded sharp Cheddar cheese

¼ cup chopped fresh cilantro (optional)

1 Preheat oven to 350°F. Spray large saucepan with nonstick cooking spray. Heat over medium-high heat. Add beef and onion. Brown beef 6 to 8 minutes, stirring to break up meat. Add beans, stewed tomatoes with juice, diced tomatoes and green chiles and chili powder. Bring to a boil. Reduce heat to low. Cover and simmer 10 minutes.

2 Place tortillas on baking sheet. Spray tortillas lightly on both sides with cooking spray. Using pizza cutter, cut each tortilla into 6 wedges. Bake 5 minutes.

3 Divide lettuce among 5 soup bowls. Ladle beef mixture evenly over lettuce. Top with cheese and cilantro, if desired. Serve with tortilla wedges.

BEEF TACO SKILLET

MAKES 4 SERVINGS | PREP TIME 5 MINUTES **COOK TIME** 20 MINUTES

1 pound ground beef

1 can (10¾ ounces) CAMPBELL'S®
    Condensed Tomato Soup
    (Regular **or** Healthy Request®)

½ cup PACE® Picante Sauce

½ cup water

6 flour tortillas (6-inch), cut into
    1-inch pieces

½ cup shredded Cheddar cheese
    (about 2 ounces)

1 Cook the beef in a 10-inch skillet over medium-high heat until well browned, stirring often to separate the meat. Pour off any fat.

2 Stir the soup, picante sauce, water and tortillas in the skillet and heat to a boil. Reduce the heat to low. Cook for 5 minutes. Stir the beef mixture. Top with the cheese.

CREAMY MEXICAN FIESTA

Stir in **½ cup** sour cream with the soup.

RANCHERO STYLE

Use corn tortillas instead of flour tortillas and shredded Mexican cheese blend instead of Cheddar.

TACO POT PIE

MAKES 4 TO 6 SERVINGS

1 pound ground beef

1 packet (1¼ ounces) taco seasoning mix

¼ cup water

1 cup canned kidney beans, rinsed and drained

1 cup chopped tomatoes

¾ cup frozen corn, thawed

¾ cup frozen peas, thawed

1½ cups (6 ounces) shredded Cheddar cheese

1 can (11½ ounces) refrigerated corn breadstick dough

1 Preheat oven to 400°F. Brown beef in medium ovenproof skillet over medium-high heat 6 to 8 minutes, stirring to break up meat. Drain fat. Add seasoning mix and water to skillet. Cook over medium-low heat 3 minutes or until most liquid is absorbed, stirring occasionally.

2 Stir in beans, tomatoes, corn and peas. Cook 3 minutes or until mixture is heated through. Remove from heat; stir in cheese.

3 Unwrap breadstick dough; separate into strips. Twist strips, cutting to fit skillet. Arrange attractively over meat mixture. Press ends of dough lightly to edge of skillet to secure. Bake 15 minutes or until bread is golden brown and meat mixture is bubbly.

CHICKEN TACO CASSEROLE

MAKES 8 SERVINGS | PREP TIME 15 MINUTES **BAKE TIME** 40 MINUTES

4 cups shredded cooked chicken

2 cans (10½ ounces **each**) CAMPBELL'S® Condensed Cream of Chicken Soup (Regular **or** 98% Fat Free)

1 cup light sour cream

1 can (10 ounces) diced tomatoes with green chiles, undrained

1 can (about 15 ounces) black beans, rinsed and drained

1 packet (about 1 ounce) reduced-sodium taco seasoning mix

15 ounces tortilla chips, crushed (about 5 cups)

2 cups shredded Cheddar cheese (about 8 ounces)

1 small tomato, chopped

1 green onion, sliced (about 2 tablespoons)

1 tablespoon chopped cilantro (optional)

1 Heat the oven to 350°F. Lightly grease a 13×9×2-inch baking dish. Stir the chicken, soup, sour cream, tomatoes and green chiles, beans and seasoning mix in a large bowl.

2 Layer **half** the chicken mixture, **3 cups** tortilla chips and **half** the cheese in the baking dish. Layer with the remaining chicken mixture and tortilla chips. Cover the baking dish.

3 Bake for 30 minutes. Uncover the baking dish. Sprinkle with the remaining cheese.

4 Bake, uncovered, for 10 minutes or until hot and bubbling and the cheese is melted. Sprinkle with the chopped tomato, green onion and cilantro before serving, if desired.

TACO PIZZA

MAKES 4 SERVINGS

1 package (13.8 ounces) refrigerated pizza dough

¾ pound 93% lean ground turkey

½ cup chopped onion

1 can (8 ounces) tomato sauce

1 packet (1¼ ounces) taco seasoning mix

2 medium plum tomatoes, thinly sliced, *or* 1 cup chopped tomatoes

1 cup (4 ounces) shredded Cheddar cheese

1½ cups shredded lettuce

1 Preheat oven to 425°F. Lightly spray 12-inch pizza pan with nonstick cooking spray. Unroll pizza dough; press into prepared pan. Build up edges slightly. Prick dough with fork. Bake 7 to 10 minutes or until lightly browned.

2 Meanwhile, lightly spray large nonstick skillet with cooking spray. Add turkey and onion; cook and stir until turkey is no longer pink. Add tomato sauce and seasoning mix; bring to a boil. Reduce heat; simmer, uncovered, 2 to 3 minutes. Spoon turkey mixture on warm pizza crust. Bake 5 minutes.

3 Arrange tomatoes over of turkey mixture. Sprinkle with cheese. Bake 2 to 3 minutes more or until cheese melts. Top with lettuce. Cut into 8 pieces before serving.

MEXICAN BLACK BEAN CASSEROLE

MAKES 4 SERVINGS

1 can (about 15 ounces) black beans, rinsed and drained

1½ cups (6 ounces) shredded cooked chicken

4 large green onions, sliced

1 cup salsa

¾ cup diced tomatoes

2 teaspoons ground cumin

¾ cup (3 ounces) shredded Mexican cheese blend, divided

2 (9-inch) whole wheat flour tortillas, divided

¼ cup chopped fresh cilantro

1 Heat oven to 375°F. Place beans in large bowl; partially mash with potato masher or bottom of heavy glass. Add chicken, green onions, salsa, tomatoes and cumin; mix well. Spoon 1⅓ cups mixture into 9-inch round glass baking dish; top with ½ cup cheese. Arrange 1 tortilla over mixture, tearing to fit size of dish. Repeat layering with 1⅓ cups bean mixture, remaining tortilla and remaining bean mixture. Cover dish with foil and bake 30 minutes or until heated through.

2 Remove from oven, uncover, and top with remaining ¼ cup cheese. Return to oven and continue to bake 5 minutes or until cheese is melted. Remove from oven and top with cilantro.

LOCO LOBSTER ROLLS

MAKES 4 SANDWICHES | PREP TIME 10 MINUTES **START TO FINISH** 15 MINUTES

1 cup cooked lobster meat, chopped

¼ teaspoon celery salt

1 stalk celery, diced

¼ cup mayonnaise

2 tablespoons ORTEGA® Taco Sauce, Medium

2 tablespoons ORTEGA® Fire-Roasted Diced Green Chiles

½ cup ORTEGA® Black Beans, drained

1 packet (1 ounce) ORTEGA® Fish Taco Seasoning Mix

4 top-cut or regular hot dog rolls

2 tablespoons butter

1 cup shredded iceberg lettuce

COMBINE lobster meat, celery salt, celery, mayonnaise, taco sauce, chiles, beans and fish taco seasoning mix in medium bowl. Stir well to combine.

HEAT large skillet over medium heat. Open hot dog rolls and spread butter on inside of each. Lay the roll flat, face down in the skillet and brown, 4 minutes.

SERVE lobster mixture and shredded lettuce on warmed roll.

TIP

Substitute cooked shrimp for lobster meat to make an excellent shrimp roll.

CHA-CHA-CHA CASSEROLE

MAKES 6 SERVINGS

1 can (about 7 ounces) whole green chiles, drained

1 pound ground turkey or chicken

1 cup chopped onion

3 cloves garlic, minced

1 tablespoon chili powder

1 teaspoon salt

1 teaspoon ground cumin

1 can (about 14 ounces) diced tomatoes with green chiles

2 cups thawed frozen corn

1 can (16 ounces) refried beans

2 cups (8 ounces) shredded Mexican cheese blend

2 cups crushed tortilla chips

1 cup chopped fresh tomatoes

½ cup sliced green onions

1 Preheat oven to 375°F. Spray 8-inch square baking dish with nonstick cooking spray. Cut chiles in half lengthwise; place in single layer in prepared baking dish.

2 Lightly coat medium nonstick skillet with cooking spray; heat over medium heat. Add turkey, onion, garlic, chili powder, salt and cumin; cook and stir 5 minutes or until turkey is no longer pink. Stir in canned tomatoes; cook 10 minutes or until most of liquid evaporates, stirring occasionally.

3 Spoon turkey mixture over chiles; top with corn and beans. Sprinkle with cheese and crushed chips. Bake 30 minutes. Let stand 5 minutes. Sprinkle with fresh tomatoes and green onions just before serving.

SWIRLY NOODLE
TACO SKILLET

MAKES 6 SERVINGS | PREP TIME 5 MINUTES **START TO FINISH** 25 MINUTES

1 pound ground beef

1 onion, diced (about 1 cup)

1 packet (1.25 ounces) ORTEGA® Taco Seasoning Mix

1 can (7 ounces) ORTEGA® Fire-Roasted Diced Green Chiles

1 jar (16 ounces) ORTEGA® Salsa, any variety

½ pound rotini or fusilli pasta, uncooked

Shredded Cheddar cheese (optional)

BROWN ground beef and onion in large skillet over medium-high heat 6 to 8 minutes, stirring to break up meat. Drain fat.

ADD taco seasoning mix, chiles, salsa and 2 cups water; stir to combine. Add pasta and stir. Reduce heat to low. Cover and cook 12 to 14 minutes or until pasta is cooked through. Serve with cheese.

TIP

This dish also makes a great taco filling, for ORTEGA® Yellow Corn Taco Shells or soft flour tortillas.

TACO CASSEROLE

MAKES 4 TO 6 SERVINGS

2 pounds ground beef

1 can (10 ounces) diced tomatoes with green chiles

1 teaspoon salt

1 teaspoon garlic powder

1 teaspoon ground cumin

1 teaspoon paprika

1 teaspoon chili powder

½ teaspoon ground red pepper

½ teaspoon red pepper flakes

1 bag (12 ounces) nacho-cheese flavored tortilla chips, crushed

½ cup chopped green onions

1 cup (4 ounces) shredded Mexican cheese blend

½ cup sour cream (optional)

1 Preheat oven to 375°F.

2 Brown beef in large skillet over medium-high heat 6 to 8 minutes, stirring to break up meat. Drain fat. Stir in tomatoes, salt, garlic powder, cumin, paprika, chili powder, ground red pepper and red pepper flakes; cook 3 minutes.

3 Stir in chips. Transfer to 13×9-inch casserole.

4 Bake 15 to 20 minutes or until heated through. Sprinkle with green onions and cheese. Serve with sour cream, if desired.

SIMPLE SIDES

MEXICAN-STYLE CORN ON THE COB

MAKES 4 SERVINGS

2 tablespoons reduced-fat mayonnaise

½ teaspoon chili powder

½ teaspoon grated lime peel

4 ears corn, shucked

2 tablespoons grated Parmesan cheese

1 Prepare grill for direct cooking. Combine mayonnaise, chili powder and lime peel in small bowl; set aside.

2 Grill corn over medium-high heat, uncovered, 4 to 6 minutes or until lightly charred, turning 3 times. Immediately spread mayonnaise mixture over corn. Sprinkle with cheese.

QUICK GREENS AND BEANS

MAKES 4 SERVINGS | PREP TIME 5 MINUTES **START TO FINISH** 15 MINUTES

- 3 slices bacon, diced
- 5 collard leaves, stems removed, chopped
- ½ cup ORTEGA® Black Beans, rinsed, drained

- 2 tablespoons ORTEGA® Fire-Roasted Diced Green Chiles
- 2 tablespoons ORTEGA® Taco Sauce, any variety
- Salt and black pepper, to taste

COOK bacon in medium skillet over medium-high heat until crispy. Meanwhile, bring small saucepan of salted water to a boil. Stir in collard leaves. Boil 5 minutes. Drain; add to bacon in skillet. Stir in black beans, chiles and taco sauce. Add salt and pepper to taste; toss to combine well.

NOTE

You can replace the black beans with pinto or kidney beans, or add corn for extra color.

MEXICAN MASHED POTATOES

MAKES 6 SERVINGS | PREP TIME 5 MINUTES **START TO FINISH** 25 MINUTES

- 3 pounds russet potatoes, peeled and diced
- 4 tablespoons (½ stick) butter
- ¼ cup milk

- 1 can (4 ounces) ORTEGA® Fire-Roasted Diced Green Chiles
- Salt and black pepper, to taste
- 1 packet (1.25 ounces) ORTEGA® Taco Seasoning Mix

BRING large saucepot of salted water to a boil. Add potatoes. Cook 10 minutes or until soft. Drain water from pot.

ADD butter, milk, chiles, salt and pepper to taste. Mash well. Stir in seasoning mix. Serve warm.

TIP

For an even richer side dish, stir in 1 cup shredded Cheddar or Monterey Jack cheese.

SIMPLE SIDES

TORTILLA SOUP

MAKES 4 SERVINGS

Vegetable oil

3 (6- or 7-inch) corn tortillas, halved and cut into strips

½ cup chopped onion

1 clove garlic, minced

2 cans (about 14 ounces each) chicken broth

1 can (about 14 ounces) diced tomatoes

1 cup shredded cooked chicken

2 teaspoons fresh lime juice

1 small avocado, diced

2 tablespoons fresh cilantro

1 Pour oil to depth of ½ inch in small skillet. Heat over medium-high heat until oil reaches 360°F on deep-fry thermometer. Add tortilla strips, a few at a time, fry 1 minute or until crisp and lightly browned. Remove with slotted spoon; drain on paper towels.

2 Heat 2 teaspoons oil in large saucepan over medium heat. Add onion and garlic; cook and stir until onion is soft. Add broth and tomatoes; bring to a boil. Cover; reduce heat and simmer 15 minutes.

3 Add chicken and lime juice; simmer 5 minutes. Top soup with tortilla strips, avocado and cilantro.

SPICY SWEET POTATO FRIES WITH CREAMY CHILI DIPPING SAUCE

MAKES 3 TO 5 SERVINGS | PREP TIME 5 MINUTES **START TO FINISH** 25 MINUTES

3 large sweet potatoes, peeled, sliced into ½-inch strips

2 tablespoons cornstarch

2 tablespoons olive oil

1 packet (1.25 ounces) ORTEGA® Taco Seasoning Mix,* divided

1 cup sour cream

2 tablespoons ORTEGA® Taco Sauce, any variety

For a healthier alternative, try ORTEGA® 40% Reduced Sodium Taco Seasoning Mix.

PREHEAT oven to 400°F.

PLACE potato strips in large bowl. Sprinkle with cornstarch; toss until evenly coated. Drizzle oil over potatoes; toss until evenly coated. Add all but 1 tablespoon seasoning mix; toss until evenly coated.

ARRANGE potato strips on two ungreased baking sheets; potato strips should touch.

BAKE 20 minutes or until done and lightly browned.

COMBINE sour cream, taco sauce and remaining 1 tablespoon seasoning mix in small bowl; mix well.

SERVE potatoes immediately with Creamy Chili Dipping Sauce.

LAYERED MEXICAN SALAD

MAKES 8 SERVINGS

1 package (10 ounces) shredded lettuce

½ cup chopped green onions (green and white parts)

½ cup sour cream

⅓ cup medium picante sauce

1 medium lime, halved

1 teaspoon sugar

½ teaspoon ground cumin

1 medium avocado, chopped

¾ cup (3 ounces) shredded sharp Cheddar cheese

2 ounces baked tortilla chips, coarsely crumbled

1 Place lettuce evenly in 13×9-inch baking dish. Sprinkle with green onions.

2 Stir together sour cream, picante sauce, juice from half of lime, sugar and cumin in small bowl. Spoon evenly over lettuce and green onions. Place avocado evenly over sour cream layer. Squeeze remaining lime half evenly over avocado layer. Sprinkle evenly with cheese.

3 Cover with plastic wrap. Refrigerate until serving. (May be prepared 8 hours in advance, if desired.) Sprinkle with crumbled tortilla chips before serving.

VARIATION

Add chopped fresh tomatoes to avocado layer.
Sprinkle chip layer with chopped fresh cilantro.

SALSA VEGETABLE SOUP WITH FIESTA FLATS CROUTONS

MAKES 6 TO 8 SERVINGS | PREP TIME 10 MINUTES **START TO FINISH** 50 MINUTES

2 tablespoons olive oil

1 onion, diced

1 carrot, peeled and diced

1 green bell pepper, diced

2 cloves garlic, minced

1 zucchini, diced

1 packet (1.25 ounces) ORTEGA® Taco Seasoning Mix

1 can (15 ounces) ORTEGA® Black Beans with Jalapeños

1 can (7 ounces) ORTEGA® Fire-Roasted Diced Green Chiles

2 jars (16 ounces each) ORTEGA® Black Bean and Corn Salsa

½ cup frozen corn

Salt and black pepper, to taste

6 ORTEGA® Fiesta Flats Flat Bottom Taco Shells

HEAT oil in large stockpot over medium heat. Add onion, carrot, bell pepper and garlic; cook 5 minutes or until vegetables begin to soften.

ADD zucchini, taco seasoning mix, beans, chiles and salsa. Stir to combine. Add 1 salsa jar of water to the pot. Bring to a boil; reduce heat to simmer and cook 30 minutes.

ADD corn; continue to cook 10 minutes. Season with salt and black pepper. Serve soup in bowls garnished with Fiesta Flats as corn "croutons."

TIP

This dish can easily be chilled and served as a summer gazpacho-type soup.

MEXICAN SLAW

MAKES 8 SERVINGS

1 (6-inch) corn tortilla, cut into thin strips

¼ teaspoon chili powder

3 cups shredded green cabbage

1 cup shredded red cabbage

½ cup shredded carrots

½ cup sliced radishes

½ cup corn

¼ cup coarsely chopped fresh cilantro

¼ cup mayonnaise

1 tablespoon fresh lime juice

2 teaspoons cider vinegar

1 teaspoon honey

½ teaspoon ground cumin

¼ teaspoon salt

¼ teaspoon black pepper

1 Preheat oven to 350°F. Arrange tortilla strips in even layer on nonstick baking sheet. Spray strips with nonstick cooking spray and sprinkle with chili powder. Bake 6 to 8 minutes or until crisp.

2 Combine cabbage, carrots, radishes, corn and cilantro in large bowl. Combine mayonnaise, lime juice, vinegar, honey, cumin, salt and pepper in small bowl. Add mayonnaise mixture to cabbage mixture; toss gently to coat. Top with baked tortilla strips.

ROASTED TACO CAULIFLOWER

MAKES 4 TO 6 SERVINGS | PREP TIME 10 MINUTES **START TO FINISH** 35 MINUTES

1 head cauliflower, cut into florets

2 tablespoons olive oil

1 packet (1.25 ounces) ORTEGA®
Taco Seasoning Mix or 40% Less
Sodium Taco Seasoning Mix

PREHEAT oven to 425°F.

PLACE cauliflower on large rimmed baking sheet. Drizzle oil over cauliflower and sprinkle with seasoning mix; toss to coat evenly.

BAKE 25 minutes or until cauliflower is tender. Serve warm.

TIP

ORTEGA® Taco Seasoning Mix also adds great flavor to other roasted vegetables, such as carrots, turnips or Brussels sprouts. Prepare as directed.

BROILED
TACO-STUFFED TOMATOES

MAKES 4 SERVINGS | PREP TIME 10 MINUTES **START TO FINISH** 15 MINUTES

- 4 small ripe plum tomatoes
- 3 ORTEGA® Yellow Corn Taco Shells
- ½ cup ORTEGA® Salsa, any variety
- ½ cup grated Parmesan cheese
- 1 teaspoon MRS. DASH® Italian Medley Seasoning Blend

CUT small slice from opposite sides of tomatoes; cut crosswise in half. Scoop out and discard pulp. Place tomato shells on small baking sheet.

PREHEAT broiler on low.

BREAK taco shells into food processor and pulse several times to create about ½ cup finely ground crumbs. Place in medium bowl. Stir in salsa, cheese and seasoning; mix well.

DIVIDE taco mixture among tomato shells, pressing down with fingertips to stuff well.

BROIL 6 inches from heat about 5 minutes or until lightly browned on top.

SIMPLE SIDES

FIESTA CORN SALAD

MAKES 4 TO 6 SERVINGS

5 large ears fresh corn

Fiesta Dressing (recipe follows)

1½ cups shredded red cabbage

1 large tomato, chopped

1 medium green bell pepper, seeded and chopped

5 slices bacon, cooked and crumbled (optional)

1 cup coarsely crushed tortilla chips

1 cup (4 ounces) shredded Cheddar cheese

Remove husks and silk from corn. Place in boiling water; cover. Cook 6 minutes or until tender; drain. Cool. Meanwhile prepare Fiesta Dressing. Cut corn from cob using sharp knife. Combine corn, cabbage, tomato and pepper in large bowl. Pour dressing over vegetables; mix lightly. Cover; refrigerate. Stir in bacon just before serving, if desired. Spoon salad into large bowl; sprinkle with chips and cheese.

FIESTA DRESSING

MAKES 1 CUP

1 cup plain yogurt

3 tablespoons minced onion

1½ tablespoons fresh lime juice

1 clove garlic, minced

1 teaspoon ground cumin

1 teaspoon chili powder

¼ teaspoon salt

Combine ingredients in small bowl; mix well.

TACO BREADED ZUCCHINI

MAKES 4 SERVINGS | PREP TIME 5 MINUTES **START TO FINISH** 15 MINUTES

8 ORTEGA® Yellow Corn Taco Shells

1 egg, slightly beaten

1 packet (1.25 ounces) ORTEGA® Taco Seasoning Mix

1 cup all-purpose flour

¼ cup vegetable oil

2 zucchini, sliced into ¼-inch rings

PLACE taco shells in food processor; pulse several minutes until shells are size of large bread crumbs. Pour into shallow pie pan.

BEAT egg in second shallow pie pan. Combine taco seasoning mix and flour in third shallow pie pan.

HEAT oil in large skillet over medium heat.

DREDGE each of zucchini slices first in taco-seasoned flour, shaking off excess. Next, coat with egg and finally in crushed taco shells; set aside. Place zucchini in batches into oil; cook 4 minutes per side. Remove and drain on paper towel.

TIP

Try this preparation technique with onions rings as well.

MEXICAN TORTILLA SOUP

MAKES 8 SERVINGS

2 pounds boneless skinless chicken breasts, cut into ½-inch strips

4 cups diced carrots

2 cups sliced celery

1 cup chopped green bell pepper

1 cup chopped onion

4 cloves garlic, minced

1 jalapeño pepper,* seeded and sliced

1 teaspoon dried oregano

½ teaspoon ground cumin

8 cups chicken broth

1 large tomato, seeded and chopped

4 to 5 tablespoons fresh lime juice

2 (6-inch) corn tortillas, cut into ¼-inch strips

Salt (optional)

3 tablespoons finely chopped fresh cilantro

*Jalapeño peppers can sting and irritate the skin, so wear rubber gloves when handling peppers and do not touch your eyes.

1 Preheat oven to 350°F. Spray large nonstick Dutch oven with nonstick cooking spray; heat over medium heat. Add chicken; cook and stir 10 minutes or until browned and cooked through. Add carrots, celery, bell pepper, onion, garlic, jalapeño pepper, oregano and cumin. Cook and stir over medium heat 5 minutes.

2 Add broth, tomato and lime juice; bring to a boil. Reduce heat to low; cover and simmer 15 to 20 minutes.

3 Meanwhile, spray tortilla strips lightly with cooking spray; sprinkle lightly with salt, if desired. Place on baking sheet. Bake 10 minutes or until browned and crisp, stirring occasionally.

4 Stir cilantro into soup. Ladle soup into bowls; top evenly with tortilla strips.

MEXICAN RICE OLÉ

MAKES 4 SERVINGS

1 teaspoon vegetable oil

1 cup uncooked long grain rice

1 teaspoon salt

1 clove garlic, minced

1 can (14½ ounces) chicken broth

1 can (10¾ ounces) condensed
cream of chicken soup,
undiluted

¾ cup sour cream

1 can (4 ounces) chopped mild
green chiies, undrained

⅓ cup salsa

1 teaspoon ground cumin

1 cup (4 ounces) shredded
Cheddar cheese

1 can (about 2 ounces) sliced
black olives, drained

1 Preheat oven to 350°F. Coat 3-quart casserole with nonstick cooking spray.

2 Heat oil in large skillet over medium heat. Cook and stir rice, salt and garlic 2 to 3 minutes or until rice is well coated. Add enough water to broth to equal 2 cups. Pour into skillet and simmer, stirring occasionally, about 15 minutes or until rice is tender.

3 Remove skillet from heat and add soup, sour cream, chiles, salsa and cumin; mix well. Spoon into prepared casserole; bake 20 minutes.

4 Top with cheese and olives. Bake additional 5 to 10 minutes or until cheese melts and casserole is heated through.

SAVORY MEXICAN POTATO TART

MAKES 8 SERVINGS

3 medium russet potatoes (about 1 pound), peeled

½ cup all-purpose flour

¼ cup cornmeal

4 tablespoons vegetable oil, divided

½ teaspoon garlic salt

½ teaspoon black pepper

1 jar (8 ounces) mild taco sauce

1 medium onion, chopped

1 cup shredded cooked chicken

1 cup (4 ounces) shredded Monterey Jack cheese

1 small jalapeño pepper,* seeded and minced

2 tablespoons chopped fresh oregano

Prepared guacamole

Jalapeño peppers can sting and irritate the skin, so wear rubber gloves when handling peppers and do not touch your eyes.

1 Place potatoes in large saucepan; add enough water to cover. Bring to a boil over high heat. Reduce heat to low; cover and simmer 30 minutes or until potatoes are fork-tender. Drain. Mash potatoes in large bowl with electric mixer at low speed.

2 Preheat oven to 350°F.

3 Combine warm mashed potatoes, flour, cornmeal, 3 tablespoons oil, garlic salt and black pepper in large bowl; mix until smooth.

4 Dust hands with flour. Press potato mixture onto bottom and up side of ungreased 10-inch flan or tart pan with removable bottom; set aside.

5 Combine taco sauce with onion in small bowl; spread evenly over potato mixture. Top with chicken, cheese, jalapeño pepper and oregano. Drizzle with remaining 1 tablespoon oil.

6 Bake 30 minutes or until potato mixture is heated through. Cool in pan 10 minutes.

7 Carefully loosen edge of tart using knife. Remove rim from pan.

8 Remove potato tart from pan bottom; cut into wedges. Serve with guacamole. Garnish, if desired.

SATISFYING SWEETS

SPICY TROPICAL FRUIT SKEWERS

MAKES 8 SERVINGS | PREP TIME 10 MINUTES **START TO FINISH** 30 MINUTES

16 wooden skewers, each about 6 inches long

3 medium ripe mangos, peeled, each cut into 8 wedges, then halved crosswise

2 to 3 large kiwis, peeled, each cut into 8 wedges

1 can (20 ounces) pineapple chunks, drained

2 tablespoons ORTEGA® Taco Sauce, Hot

1 tablespoon honey

2 teaspoons grated fresh ginger

SOAK skewers in water at least 30 minutes to prevent burning.

PREHEAT grill to medium heat, about 10 minutes.

COMBINE mangos, kiwis, pineapple, taco sauce, honey and ginger in large bowl; gently toss to mix well. Let stand about 15 minutes.

THREAD fruit evenly on skewers. Grill 3 to 5 minutes, turning once and brushing with any leftover honey mixture.

TIP

Serve as a dessert with your favorite flavored yogurt or as a side dish with pork or chicken.

CREAMY DREAMY TACO TOMB TREATS

MAKES 6 SERVINGS

¼ cup plus 2 tablespoons packed light brown sugar

2 egg whites

2 tablespoons butter, melted and slightly cooled

1 teaspoon vanilla

½ teaspoon ground cinnamon

¼ teaspoon ground nutmeg

½ cup pecans or walnuts, chopped

2 tablespoons all-purpose flour

2 cups vanilla or chocolate ice cream

Fresh chopped strawberries and pineapple

Chocolate sprinkles

1 Preheat oven to 375°F.

2 Beat brown sugar, egg whites, butter, vanilla, cinnamon and nutmeg in medium bowl with electric mixer at medium speed 1 minute.

3 Combine pecans and flour in food processor; pulse until coarsely ground. Add to sugar mixture and stir until well blended. Let stand 10 minutes to thicken.

4 Spray baking sheet with nonstick cooking spray. Spoon 2 tablespoons batter onto baking sheet. Using back of spoon, spread into 5-inch circle. Repeat with another 2 tablespoons batter, placed 4 to 5 inches apart. Bake 5 minutes or until light brown. Cool on wire rack 1 minute. Gently remove each cookie with metal spatula and place over rolling pin. Let cool 5 minutes. Repeat with remaining batter.

5 Fill each cookie with ⅓ cup ice cream. Wrap in plastic wrap; freeze until ready to serve. Top with fruit and chocolate sprinkles before serving.

SATISFYING SWEETS

CINNAMON TACOS WITH FRUIT SALSA

MAKES 6 SERVINGS | PREP TIME 20 MINUTES **START TO FINISH** 30 MINUTES

1 cup sliced fresh strawberries

1 cup cubed fresh pineapple

1 cup cubed peeled kiwi

½ teaspoon ORTEGA® Diced Jalapeños

4 tablespoons plus 1 teaspoon granulated sugar, divided

1 tablespoon ground cinnamon

6 (8-inch) ORTEGA® Flour Soft Tortillas

Nonstick cooking spray

STIR together strawberries, pineapple, kiwi, jalapeños and 4 teaspoons sugar (adjust to taste, if desired) in large bowl; set aside.

COMBINE remaining 3 tablespoons sugar and cinnamon in small bowl; set aside.

COAT tortillas lightly on both sides with nonstick cooking spray. Heat each tortilla in nonstick skillet over medium heat until slightly puffed and golden brown. Remove from heat; immediately dust both sides with cinnamon-sugar mixture. Shake excess cinnamon-sugar back into bowl. Repeat cooking and dusting process until all tortillas are warmed.

FOLD tortillas in half and fill with fruit mixture. Serve immediately.

SATISFYING SWEETS

SALTED CHOCOLATE-COVERED TOSTADAS

MAKES 10 SERVINGS | PREP TIME 10 MINUTES **START TO FINISH** 40 MINUTES

¾ cup semisweet chocolate chips

2 tablespoons ORTEGA® Taco Seasoning Mix

3 tablespoons whipping cream

1 package (10-count) ORTEGA® Tostada Shells

1 teaspoon sea salt

Ice cream, any flavor (optional)

Additional ORTEGA® Taco Seasoning Mix (optional)

COMBINE chocolate chips and seasoning mix in small microwavable bowl. Microwave on HIGH 30 seconds; stir. If necessary, heat in 15-second intervals until chocolate is melted. Add cream; mix well.

SPREAD chocolate mixture onto one side of tostada shell using pastry brush; sprinkle with pinch of salt. Repeat with remaining chocolate, tostada shells and salt.

CHILL in refrigerator at least 30 minutes or until chocolate sets. If desired, place scoop of ice cream on tostada shell before serving and garnish with additional seasoning mix before serving.

TIP

You can use white, milk or dark chocolate chips to create a variety of dessert tostada shells.

CHOCOLATE MOLÉ FONDUE

MAKES 6 SERVINGS | PREP TIME 15 MINUTES **START TO FINISH** 25 MINUTES

CINNAMON CHIPS

2 tablespoons granulated sugar

2 teaspoons ground cinnamon

6 (8-inch) ORTEGA® Flour Soft Tortillas

Butter-flavored cooking spray

FONDUE

1 cup semisweet or dark chocolate chips

½ cup whipping cream

3 tablespoons ORTEGA® Taco Sauce, any variety

PREHEAT oven to 350°F. Combine sugar and cinnamon in small bowl. Set aside.

COAT one side of each tortilla with cooking spray. Cut into wedges; arrange in single layer on large baking sheet, coated side down. Sprinkle evenly with cinnamon-sugar. Spray again with cooking spray.

BAKE 8 to 10 minutes or until crisp, turning once.

COMBINE chocolate chips, whipping cream and taco sauce in small saucepan over low heat. Cook and stir until chocolate has melted and mixture is smooth.

KEEP chocolate mixture warm in small saucepan, slow cooker or fondue pot. Serve with cinnamon chips for dipping.

SWEET AND SPICY BANANAS FOSTER

MAKES 4 SERVINGS | PREP TIME 1 MINUTE **START TO FINISH** 5 MINUTES

½ cup (1 stick) butter

½ cup firmly packed light brown sugar

2 tablespoons ORTEGA® Taco Seasoning Mix

4 bananas, peeled, halved and cut in half lengthwise

¼ cup dark rum

Vanilla ice cream

MELT butter in large skillet over medium heat. Stir in brown sugar; cook and stir until smooth and sugar has dissolved. Stir in seasoning mix.

ADD banana quarters; swirl around in skillet to coat bananas completely. Add rum; simmer 4 minutes or until alcohol has cooked out.

PLACE ice cream in serving dishes. Arrange 4 banana pieces in each dish; spoon sauce over ice cream and bananas.

TIP

For a warmer treat, serve this sweet and spicy version of bananas Foster over pound cake or your favorite coffee cake.

FRUIT BURRITOS

MAKES 4 SERVINGS | PREP TIME 10 MINUTES

1 cup vanilla nonfat yogurt

½ cup SKIPPY® Creamy Peanut Butter

4 (8-inch) soft taco-size flour or whole wheat tortillas

2 cups sliced strawberries

1 cup fresh blueberries

2 teaspoons cinnamon-sugar

1 In medium bowl, combine yogurt and peanut butter; mix well.

2 Spread peanut butter mixture evenly over tortillas. Top with berries; sprinkle with cinnamon-sugar. Roll and fold filled tortillas.

TIP

For Fruit Tostadas, toast tortillas until crisp, then spread with peanut butter mixture and top as directed.

SATISFYING SWEETS

INDEX

7-Layer Dip, 12

A

Appetizers & Snacks

7-Layer Dip, 12

Bite Size Tacos, 30

Buffalo Guacamole, 34

Classic Guacamole, 16

Easy Empanadas, 18

Easy Taco Dip, 24

Festive Taco Cups, 20

Festive Taco Nachos, 22

Layered Mexican Dip, 23

Mexican Tortilla Stacks, 14

Mini Beef Tostadas, 4

Mini Taco Quiches, 10

Number One Nachos, 35

Taco Cheese Balls, 26

Taco Dip, 32

Taco Popcorn Olé, 6

Tex-Mex Guacamole Platter, 28

Tortilla "Pizzas", 8

B

Beef Taco Skillet, 132

Beer-Braised Spicy Beef Tacos, 96

Bite Size Tacos, 30

Braised Brisket Street-Style Tacos, 100

Breakfast & Brunches

Breakfast Pancake Tacos, 58

Breakfast Taco Bar, 52

Breakfast Tacos, 36

Breakfast Tamale Pie, 54

Johnsonville® Breakfast Empanadas, 50

Mexed-Up French Toast with Spiced Chocolate Drizzle, 56

Mexican Breakfast Burrito, 40

Mexican Hash Brown Bake, 48

Spanish Tortilla, 46

Spicy Mexican Frittata, 42

Tortilla Frittata, 38

Tortilla Scramble with Salsa, 44

Breakfast Pancake Tacos, 58

Breakfast Taco Bar, 52

Breakfast Tacos, 36

Breakfast Tamale Pie, 54

Broiled Taco-Stuffed Tomatoes, 163

Buffalo Guacamole, 34

C

Cha-Cha-Cha Casserole, 142

Cheesy Chicken Chili, 114

Chicken and Spicy Black Bean Tacos, 66

Chicken Taco Casserole, 136

Chilies & Soups
  Cheesy Chicken Chili, 114
  Chili in Tortilla Bowls, 104
  Hearty Chicken Chili, 122
  Mexican Tortilla Soup, 168
  Salsa Vegetable Soup with Fiesta Flats Croutons, 158
  Taco Stew, 130
  Tortilla Soup, 152

Chili in Tortilla Bowls, 104
Chipotle Taco Filling, 64
Chocolate Molé Fondue, 182
Chorizo and Papa Burritos, 112
Cinnamon Tacos with Fruit Salsa, 178
Citrus Crab Tacos with Apricot Cocktail Sauce, 80
Classic Guacamole, 16
Creamy Dreamy Taco Tomb Treats, 176
Crunchy Layered Beef & Bean Salad, 128

D
Devil's Fire Shredded Beef Tacos, 102
Double Duty Tacos, 62

E
Easy Empanadas, 18
Easy Taco Dip, 24
Easy Taco Salad, 110

Entrées & Tacos
  Beef Taco Skillet, 132
  Beer-Braised Spicy Beef Tacos, 96
  Braised Brisket Street-Style Tacos, 100

Cha-Cha-Cha Casserole, 142
Chicken and Spicy Black Bean Tacos, 66
Chicken Taco Casserole, 136
Chipotle Taco Filling, 64
Chorizo and Papa Burritos, 112
Citrus Crab Tacos with Apricot Cocktail Sauce, 80
Devil's Fire Shredded Beef Tacos, 102
Double Duty Tacos, 62
Fish Tacos with Cilantro Cream Sauce, 76
Fish Tacos with Citrus Pineapple Salsa, 94
Fish Tacos with Yogurt Sauce, 70
Loco Lobster Rolls, 140
Mexican Black Bean Casserole, 139
Mexican Casserole with Tortilla Chips, 108
Mexican Pizza, 126
Mexican Stuffed Peppers, 116
Mexican Tortilla Stack-Ups, 118
Monterey Chicken Tortilla Casserole, 124
Ramen "Spaghetti" Tacos, 86
RedHot Tacos, 88
Simple Shredded Pork Tacos, 73
Soft Tacos with Chicken, 92
Soft Turkey Tacos, 82
Southwest Buffalo Chicken Tacos, 72
Speedy Tacos, 90
Spicy Beef Tacos, 74
Spicy Burrito Burgers, 106
Spiraled Sweet Potato and Black Bean Tacos, 98
Swirly Noodle Taco Skillet, 144

Taco Casserole, 146

Taco Pizza, 138

Taco Pot Pie, 134

Taco Tater Bites, 120

Terrific Tacos, 84

Tomatillo Pork Tacos, 60

Turkey and Winter Squash Tacos, 68

Turkey Tacos, 78

F

Festive Taco Cups, 20

Festive Taco Nachos, 22

Fiesta Corn Salad, 164

Fish Tacos with Cilantro Cream Sauce, 76

Fish Tacos with Citrus Pineapple Salsa, 94

Fish Tacos with Yogurt Sauce, 70

Fruit Burritos, 188

H

Hearty Chicken Chili, 122

J

Johnsonville® Breakfast Empanadas, 50

L

Layered Mexican Dip, 23

Layered Mexican Salad, 156

Loco Lobster Rolls, 140

M

Mexed-Up French Toast with Spiced Chocolate Drizzle, 56

Mexican Black Bean Casserole, 139

Mexican Breakfast Burrito, 40

Mexican Casserole with Tortilla Chips, 108

Mexican Hash Brown Bake, 48

Mexican Mashed Potatoes, 151

Mexican Pizza, 126

Mexican Rice Olé, 170

Mexican Slaw, 160

Mexican Stuffed Peppers, 116

Mexican Tortilla Soup, 168

Mexican Tortilla Stack-Ups, 118

Mexican Tortilla Stacks, 14

Mexican-Style Corn on the Cob, 148

Mini Beef Tostadas, 4

Mini Taco Quiches, 10

Monterey Chicken Tortilla Casserole, 124

N

Number One Nachos, 35

Q

Quick Greens and Beans, 150

R

Ramen "Spaghetti" Tacos, 86

RedHot Tacos, 88

Roasted Taco Cauliflower, 162

S

Salads & Sides

Broiled Taco-Stuffed Tomatoes, 163

Crunchy Layered Beef & Bean Salad, 128

Easy Taco Salad, 110

Fiesta Corn Salad, 164

Layered Mexican Salad, 156

Mexican Mashed Potatoes, 151

Mexican Rice Olé, 170

Mexican Slaw, 160

Mexican-Style Corn on the Cob, 148

Quick Greens and Beans, 150

Roasted Taco Cauliflower, 162

Savory Mexican Potato Tart, 172

Spicy Sweet Potato Fries with Creamy Chili Dipping Sauce, 154

Taco Breaded Zucchini, 166

Salsa Vegetable Soup with Fiesta Flats Croutons, 158

Salted Chocolate-Covered Tostadas, 180

Savory Mexican Potato Tart, 172

Simple Shredded Pork Tacos, 73

Soft Tacos with Chicken, 92

Soft Turkey Tacos, 82

Southwest Buffalo Chicken Tacos, 72

Spanish Tortilla, 46

Speedy Tacos, 90

Spicy Beef Tacos, 74

Spicy Burrito Burgers, 106

Spicy Mexican Frittata, 42

Spicy Sweet Potato Fries with Creamy Chili Dipping Sauce, 154

Spicy Tropical Fruit Skewers, 174

Spiraled Sweet Potato and Black Bean Tacos, 98

Sweet and Spicy Bananas Foster, 184

Sweets & Treats

Chocolate Molé Fondue, 182

Cinnamon Tacos with Fruit Salsa, 178

Creamy Dreamy Taco Tomb Treats, 176

Fruit Burritos, 188

Salted Chocolate-Covered Tostadas, 180

Spicy Tropical Fruit Skewers, 174

Sweet and Spicy Bananas Foster, 184

Swirly Noodle Taco Skillet, 144

T

Taco Breaded Zucchini, 166

Taco Casserole, 146

Taco Cheese Balls, 26

Taco Dip, 32

Taco Pizza, 138

Taco Popcorn Olé, 6

Taco Pot Pie, 134

Taco Stew, 130

Taco Tater Bites, 120

Terrific Tacos, 84

Tex-Mex Guacamole Platter, 28

Tomatillo Pork Tacos, 60

Tortilla "Pizzas", 8

Tortilla Frittata, 38

Tortilla Scramble with Salsa, 44

Tortilla Soup, 152

Turkey and Winter Squash Tacos, 68

Turkey Tacos, 78